CONQUERING SHIFTS

"I can think of no better business to be in than helping families fulfill their dream of homeownership. And to do it well makes the journey for any Mortgage Professional fulfilling, rewarding and profitable.

I have had the pleasure of sharing success principles with tens of thousands of mortgage professionals over the years and I can say with absolute certainty, success is a choice. Every Mortgage Professional featured in *Conquering Shifts* made the choice to build their "business by design", something that I have been teaching since 1992. They followed a plan. They honed their skills. They defeated the fear and threat of failing by becoming best in class. And they rose to the top with big dreams, hard work, constant learning, and a passion to serve.

The tips, strategies, concepts, and tactics will take years off your learning curve if you are new. If you are more experienced and yet yearn for more, it will help you sharpen your skills and give you higher levels of success and significance. *Conquering Shifts* is a compelling read that will take years off your learning curve, accelerate your success and give you the life and business of your dreams. Trust it!"

—**TODD M. DUNCAN,** *New York Times* bestselling author of *High Trust Selling and Time Traps*

"This well-crafted book is filled with real mortgage history, inspiration, and bulletproof tactics from some of the industry's legends. Whether you're new to the mortgage industry or looking to revitalize your practice, *Conquering Shifts* will inspire you to reach as high as you aspire to go."

—**DANIEL HARKAVY,** CEO, Building Champions, Inc., and bestselling author of
Living Forward: A Proven Plan to Stop Drifting and Get the Life You Want and
Becoming a Coaching Leader: The Proven Strategy for Building Your Own Team of Champions

"*Conquering Shifts* is a fascinating and in-depth review of highly successful mortgage originators across the country who have found the secret formula for massive success in mortgage lending. It should be required reading for anyone entering the residential mortgage lending industry! From using this book as an instructional manual of sorts to be well prepared for a great career in mortgage origination to helping current mortgage originators who desire to grow and greatly improve their skill set, this book is a treasure trove of great and proven ideas. It provides an untapped goldmine of success stories that can be used as a roadmap to origination success. It has been reported that Will Rogers once said, 'People change, but not much!' Well, this book provides numerous examples of several mortgage professionals who made the often difficult decision to make necessary changes to grow and win in their careers. I highly recommend this book to anyone remotely interested in our industry!"

—L. H. "MIKE" HARDWICK, III, banker, author of *Keep Chopping Wood*, entrepreneur, and proud husband and father

"*Conquering Shifts* is a must read for anyone looking to learn from the best of the best who share what it took to rise to the top of their field."

—DEBBIE ALLEN, The Market Positioning Expert, international business & brand strategist, and author of eight bestselling books.

"I thoroughly enjoyed reading this book. The authors have done an outstanding job of presenting valuable information from true icons in the lending industry. Reading this treatise is a must for loan originators, novice, and experienced.

When you start to read, allow yourself some time, for you will keep turning pages. The authors obviously are talented interviewers, researchers, and writers, and the book reflects their expertise.

So many tips, ideas, recommendations, suggestions, and so much background in every chapter.

Thank you, Cindy Douglas and Kathleen Heck, for your efforts and of course, a true thanks to the interviewees for taking the time from their extremely busy careers to help others. See you at the closings."

—DUANE GOMER, NMLS and California State Approved Course Provider for MLOs, real estate agents, and notaries

"At this point in my life, I am all about helping people through tragedy, crises, health problems and other roadblocks most of us face in life. *Conquering Shifts* has a lot of that sentiment in it. Sometimes people just need to get a helping hand or a general roadmap from someone who has already walked the path. That help is all through this book and there are roadblocks for seemingly every path in the mortgage industry. I'm not directly in that line of work, but I'm close enough to know this one will help a ton of people, by example, by suggestion, or by general motivation. I recommend it for all the people you know in the mortgage biz."

—ROSEANN C. DIAMOND, CEO, Diamond Settlement Services and author of
Holding My Hands and Saving My Life

"*Conquering Shifts* is another great guide for mortgage sales professionals who want to excel. Everyone succeeds using different versions of the same effective processes. This book includes many of those processes—finding new referral sources, offering better solutions for clients, focusing on current trends, creating value, and focusing on strengths. Some of the interviewees' stories should inspire sales people to jump out of their comfort zone and create some demand among their customers.

—PAT SHERLOCK, founder, QFS Sales Solutions, and author of *Reaching the Top of Your Game*

"Cindy Douglas has done a masterful job of both selecting and interviewing a variety of experts from different regions, who possess different skill sets, and who face different challenges from different positions, to illustrate there is always a way to win. What makes *Conquering Shifts* truly unique is that instead of simply teaching success principles or techniques, the reader gets the opportunity to see EXACTLY how they have been implemented. Like myself, most of the experts interviewed reference learning their strategies and principles from Todd Duncan, yet the way those strategies and principles have been crafted to match each individual's personality, style, or preference is truly remarkable." —MARTY PRESTON, Benchmark Mortgage

"If I were to have read this book when I first began originating purchase loans in 2011, I can honestly say that I would be leaps and bounds ahead of where I am today. *Conquering Shifts* touches on every important aspect of running a successful origination platform and it's all told by some of the most respected and tenured originators in the country. I am definitely going to be using this book to continue to refine and improve our mortgage practice, and it gives me a lot of confidence in being able to handle the inevitable and constant shifts in our market. I highly recommend not only reading but studying, this book if you want to grow your business and always be ahead of the competition!"

—**RYAN GRANT,** The Ryan Grant Team, A Professional Mortgage Practice

"These are sound practices and simple to adopt. It's great that there is now a compilation so other loan officers can pick and choose what will work best for them."

—**ALICE MORRIS,** retired mortgage sales executive

CONQUERING

SHIFTS

Cindy Douglas & Kathleen Heck

C O N Q U E R I N G

SHIFTS

Insights from

TOP MORTGAGE SALES PROFESSIONALS

CREST SPARTA
— BOOKS —

Printed in the United States
First Printing, 2018

Because of the dynamic nature of the Internet, any web address links contained in this book may have changed since the publication of this book and may no longer be valid. The views expressed in this work are do not necessarily reflect the views of the publisher, and the publisher hereby disclaims any responsibility for them.

Library of Congress Control Number: 2017918772

ISBN: 978-0-9997037-0-0 (paperback)
ISBN: 978-0-9997037-2-4 (hardback)
ISBN: 978-0-9997037-1-7 (EPub)
ISBN: 978-0-9997037-1-7 (Mobi)

Cover and interior design: Marisa Jackson

Table 1, page 136: Reprinted with permission of Tom Ninness
Table 2, page 140: Reprinted with permission of Tom Ninness

Published by Crest Sparta Books
P.O. Box 3366
Crestline, CA 92325-3366

CREST SPARTA
— BOOKS —

HERE FOLLOWS the easiest part of writing this book, the dedication. To Greg Frost, Drew McKenzie, David Jaffe, Jeff Lake, Julie Miller, Larry Bettag, Michael Deery, Mike Smalley, Ralph Massella, Tom Ninness, Mark Raskin, Karen Deis and your families, thank you. Yes, thank you for making the time for us to interview you several times. Thank you for sharing your tips, ideas, and success stories with our readers. Thank you for caring about your clients, your companies, your careers, your families, and your teams.

It's been an honor and a privilege spending time with you. We dedicate this book to you, the top and very good salespeople in the mortgage business.

In the words of Sheryl Sandberg, "If you're offered a seat on a rocket ship, don't ask what seat! Just get on."

We appreciate your allowing us to take a short part of your rocket ship ride with you. May you continue to fly above the others!

CONTENTS

THE MORTGAGE CRISIS REVISITED

―※―

> You know Americans are obsessed with life and death and rebirth,
> that's the American Cycle. You know, awakening, tragic,
> horrible death and then Phoenix rising from the ashes.
> That's the American story, again and again.
>
> —BILLY CORGAN

AS HUMAN BEINGS, we move from one life shift to another. That is also true of businesses. The companies that conquer these shifts are the Phoenix companies, rising from the ashes, again and again. The mortgage industry has seen many players come and go, with more than its share of ashes, and only a few attaining Phoenix stature.

This book focuses primarily on the most *recent* need to shift—the mortgage crisis that officially lasted from December 2007 through June 2009, and how the top performers featured in this book were able to fare so well during and after. Don't be fooled into thinking this most recent financial collapse is a modern-day phenomenon. Oh no. There have been other similar and cataclysmic events in the land of banking and home financing. Let's take a short trip down memory lane to revisit just a few of them, starting with the international panics pre-1900:

- The Panic of 1819 persisted through 1821 as the nation transitioned from its dependence on European trade to becoming more self-sufficient. This period is often referred to by many economists as the first American Housing Bust. The United States entered a recession accompanied by bank failures. The public lost confidence, a theme that recurs frequently in the various financial crises that have occurred through out history.

- The Banking Panic of 1825 was a stock market crash that originated with the Bank of England. The cause was partly due to speculative investments in Latin America. This along with numerous banks making risky loans, caused a ripple effect that was also felt in the European, North and South American financial markets. A freeze in lending triggered a six-year recession in the United States.

- The Panic of 1837 resulted from speculative lending practices in the Western United States. Contributing factors included a collapsing land bubble caused in part by declining cotton prices, and Great Britain's restricted lending policies. To stave off a domestic financial disaster, President Andrew Jackson issued an executive order known as the Specie Circular. Under this act, all land purchases were to be paid with gold or silver, which was in short supply. All these events led a to seven-year recession littered with bank failures.

- The Panic of 1847 was triggered by the collapse of the British markets in conjunction with the over-speculation into railroad stock.

- Several events contributed to the Panic of 1857. The international economy was on the decline. The railroads were heavily leveraged and unable to pay their debts. Investors were losing considerably in the stock market. The impact of these events didn't dissipate until the conclusion of the Civil War in 1865.

- The Panic of 1866 was an international financial downturn that accompanied the failure of Overend, Gurney and Company in London, England. The bank acted as the guarantor for the negotiable instruments they bought and sold. The concept was innovative for the times and expanded rapidly; however, their portfolio was unbalanced, which resulted in a lack of liquidity. Because the company was an international player, their downfall affected many nations including the United States.

- The Panic of 1873 triggered a depression in both the United States and Europe. America was still immersed in an overabundance of speculative investments that were highly concentrated in railroad stock. Inflation continued to run rampant until the end of the war. In Europe, Germany had demonetized silver to the point that the supply far outweighed the consumer's demand. And in Britain, rapidly falling grain prices caused an agricultural depression.

  The combination of these events, in conjunction with some others that were not as significant, led to what was originally known as the Great Depression. Some experts believe the depression lasted from 1873–1879, while others are of the opinion it had a longer run, ending in 1896. Those who foster the latter sentiment include the Panic of 1884, the Panic of 1890, and the Australian Banking Crisis of 1893 in their timeline. The name was officially changed in 1933, to the Long Depression. The global markets were impacted for this thirty-year period. In comparison to previous and subsequent decades, this was a time of stifled economic growth.

- The Panic of 1884 was a direct result of Europe's depleted gold reserves. The New York City national banks, with the implied blessing of the United States Treasury, called in all their outstanding loans. This, along with the failure of two major investment firms, created a domino effect. The American people had once again lost confidence in Wall Street.

- The Panic of 1890 stemmed from the Reading Railroad going into receivership, causing hundreds of businesses that relied on the railroad for their existence to fail. As the United States financial market weakened, foreign investors became skittish. The lack of confidence both domestically and internationally was in part what caused the stock market to plummet. A serious economic recession began in 1893 lasting until 1897. During this period nearly half of the banks in the United States crashed. Unemployment reached 10 percent—close to the same levels we saw during the Great Recession. (2007–2009)

- The Australian Banking Crisis of 1893 occurred when eleven high-profile commercial banks located within the continent collapsed. There were few legal restrictions and safeguards in place. All trading activity was suspended on January 30.

As America entered into the last century, there were other times our economy suffered from domestic and international events. Here are a few that are worth highlighting:

- The Post-World War I Depression of 1920–1921 occurred fourteen months after the war, leaving America in a sharp deflationary recession. High unemployment rates caused in part by the influx of soldiers returning home, along with increased government spending, contributed to the situation. However, by 1922, the economy had recovered and was once again booming.

- The Great Depression of 1930–1939, had many contributing factors, but the five major ones that stand out: (1) The 1929 Wall Street Crash, also known as "Black Tuesday"; (2) Followed immediately by 700 bank failures with an additional 2,300 closing the following year; (3) The Smoot-Hawley Tariff, which unexpectedly cut the United States international trade by two-thirds; (4) Unemployment had risen to 25 percent. Numerous families found themselves broke with their investments near, if not completely worthless. This led to an unprecedented number of repossessions and foreclosures; and (5) Severe dust storms that wasted prairie farmlands, known as the Dust Bowl which lasted from 1931–1939.

- The stock market crash of 1987, also known as "Black Monday," began in Hong Kong and spread throughout the world. On that day,

October 19, the DOW Jones industrial average plummeted almost 23 percent, or nearly 500 points. Regulators created new reforms adding more safeguards with hopes of preventing a situation of this magnitude from happening in the future.

* The 1986–1996 Savings and Loan Crisis was one of the largest bank collapses our nation has ever seen. More than half the country's savings and loans failed, resulting in $160 billion in losses. The taxpayers covered the brunt of the cost at $132 billion. The Federal Savings & Loan Insurance Corporation (FSLIC) absorbed the remaining balance of $30 billion. The crisis virtually eliminated a sound source of mortgage financing.

And moving into this century, we've seen:

* The Dotcom Bust (one of its many names) lasted from 2000–2002, which was the result of excessive speculation in the Internet and technology industries. Venture capitalists abandoned caution with the expectation of a big payday. In September of 2002, the NASDAQ lost 78 percent of its value compared to the month before, dropping it to 1,110. One month later, panic selling ensued when leading high-tech companies such as Cisco and Dell placed huge sell orders on their stock in October.

* The Financial Crisis of 2007–2008 is considered by many to be the worst economic crisis since the Great Depression. Some blame exotic mortgages with risky features while others believe the Gramm Leach Bliley Act (GLB), also known as the 1999 Financial Services Modernization Act, was the cause. GLB made it possible for investment bankers, savings and loans, and insurance companies to legally consolidate. Those against the act felt it cleared the way for these entities to become too big to fail.

Every one of the events we have covered briefly has affected the mortgage or banking industry. Each directly impacted the consumer's ability to purchase, refinance, or construct new homes. From interest rate volatility, to corporate and personal bankruptcy, to foreclosure and job losses.

Now let's turn our focus to the stars of our book who faced and successfully powered through The Great Recession of 2007–2009. A period that economists estimate household wealth in the United States dropped somewhere in the range of $16–$20 trillion, depending on whose opinion you give the most validity. Unemployment rates rose as high as 10–12 percent in some markets.

Since the crisis, American workers earn an average of 17 percent less than they would have in similar jobs beforehand. Imports, exports, and investments have declined dramatically internationally. Tens of millions of people have stayed at or fallen below the poverty line on a global level. Workers who hold jobs in industries related to housing—builders, wood product manufacturers, real estate agents, moving companies, landscapers, bankers, and, yes, mortgage loan officers—were faced with the option to shift or fall by the wayside.

Our story is about those who conquered the shifts going on around them. They didn't just survive. They were able to surpass what appeared to be insurmountable odds and achieve great success. We hope their stories inspire you to do the same.

INTRODUCTION

––––––––––––– ❊ –––––––––––––

ANYONE WHO'S BEEN in the mortgage business for any length of time has encountered periods when the economy is booming, home sales are high, and making money is great fun. It's as though the greenbacks are printing fluidly in the basement. But our industry is cyclical in nature, so we also encounter the opposite. That's when the lean years creep in and it's a struggle to keep *every single deal* from falling apart.

We can't control the economy or the decisions of political and industry leaders who believe they have the interests of the public at heart. We can, however, take preventative steps to minimize the peaks and valleys that can occur due to forces beyond our control. Learning how to recognize the signs of an economic downturn and its potential impact is critical to building a thriving practice. Embracing activities that are recession proof isn't a nicety, but a necessity. In this book, we'll try to help you course correct when the warning signs appear by illustrating what has worked for others.

Almost everything in our daily lives demands a system. Ignoring this elemental truth can create tremendous stress. Military personnel can attest to this. All aspects of their jobs require sticking to the guidelines, practicing the plan, and delivering the expected outcome. Half-baked efforts aren't acceptable because the result could be deadly. Similarly, although clearly not on the same scale, the mortgage industry tends to be fraught with never-ending battles. Often, only those who've remained true to their purpose, with focus and tenacity, have won.

Let's focus in on that win. It's not just about surviving the battle; it's about living a life of contentment and prosperity. Our definition of winning does *not* hold true for many of the thousands of originators we've collectively hired, consulted, mentored, and coached. Why? Because they lacked purpose and, as a result, weren't aligned with what was most important to them. Many operated without strategies, had knowledge deficiencies, winged it, or followed someone else's marching orders and, as a result, found themselves knee-deep in personal chaos during the mortgage meltdown.

The years of the Great Recession created a barrier between the lending community and the consumers they were trying to serve. Politicians built their campaigns on lending reform, resulting in a lot more paperwork and effort for lenders, with an increased level of distrust from the public. In the decade that's followed, the mortgage industry has lost some qualified people. We believe it's because they were blindsided by outside forces, had broken systems, stopped having fun, or a combination of these possibilities.

For those still standing after the greatest financial crisis since the Depression, we must continue to remember the lessons we've all been so painfully taught. Those who were fortunate enough not to have lived through those times can benefit from those who did. Throughout this book, you'll find stories from the Phoenix players who have weathered the storms. They succeeded then, and continue to do so.

Staying true to themselves and their passion for helping others separated them from the packs of competitors they encountered along the way. Regardless of whether these individuals faced the double-digit interest rates of the '80s, military base closures in the '90s or, most recently, the 2007–2009 mortgage crisis each one of them has continued to prosper. They found a way to turn an extremely difficult climate into opportunity, adjusting their business model and strategies as needed. You'll be surprised when you see part of you or *what could be you* in some or all of them. See what their journey can tell you about your own.

During the last thirty-plus years, we've had the pleasure of working with the best of the best and we want to share what we've learned with you. That's why we've written this book. The question isn't whether you can make money in the mortgage industry. It's whether or not you believe enough in yourself to propel forward. Are you ready to unleash your superstar? We believe you are. That's why you purchased this book.

In short, read this book and then *improve* upon the disciplines and innovations that you know without a doubt work when followed with consistent regularity. This will enable you to reach new heights in your career. Read this book to see how others did just that. Then adapt and implement the methods you can relate to.

Taking it one step further, and just as critical, we highly recommend you spend the time pinpointing what you really love to do. If you're unsure, pay attention to the choices you make both personally and professionally. A clear picture will begin to develop. We encourage you to visit our website www.conqueringshifts.com to learn more about the power of our assessment tools. Leverage your talents, inspire your team, and boost performance to fast track your success.

KLEENEX FOR MILLIONS: SALES MATH

Told to and shared by Cindy

————◆※◆————

Pure mathematics is, in its way, the poetry of logical ideas.

—ALBERT EINSTEIN

TIMELINE	EMPLOYER	ROLE
During the 2007–2008 Financial Crisis	First Magnus Mortgage	VP Training Manager
Present Employer 2017	Primary Residential Mortgage Inc.	VP National Training Division President

MANY YEARS AGO, I attended Sales Mastery,™ a retreat held by Todd Duncan in Lanai, Hawaii. At the time, expected attendance was close to one hundred. However, due to the market correction going on in 1993, many canceled at the last minute. We numbered only twenty-eight, including spouses. To this day, I consider my time in Lanai, at this *particular* event, a key turning point in my career. I met many of my closest friends and esteemed colleagues there. It was also where I met the very charismatic and charming

Greg Frost. I had heard Greg speak at several mortgage banking and broker association events previously, but I hadn't met him in person. To me, he was bigger than life, and I fully expected to be completely intimidated. While I was a big fish in my own small pond, I barely rated as a guppy next to the likes of Greg.

Todd's event encouraged networking. Because there were not a lot of activities away from the hotel, the entire group congregated at the pool, after our structured time in the morning. We discussed how our operations ran, picked one another's brains, and talked about what was important to us. We also engaged in idle chitchat that's not necessarily deep but goes a long way to solidifying friendships. It was during these gatherings that I began to know Greg and his lovely wife, Devon.

For those who haven't met him, Greg's kept his college-football physique. The tone and cadence of his voice captures the attention of those within hearing distance. Simply put, Greg has a very commanding presence. That might partially explain the phenomenal success he has attained, but the reality is these components are just icing on the cake. Greg is a numbers person, a stickler for detail. He likes to start with the end result in mind. That's how he became successful and why he has maintained continual, sustainable growth.

PERSISTENCE PAYS OFF

When I interviewed Greg for this chapter, one of the things he shared was how he got into the mortgage industry. In 1972, while finishing college and working at the Soda Straw in Albuquerque, New Mexico he became friends with a fellow co-worker. Both young men thought there had to be more to life than making shakes and serving soda. But what exactly? One day, his co-worker mentioned that his dad, Bill Burks, was the president of a local savings and loan. He was looking to fill a position for a manager trainee. Greg asked for his dad's business card and then, proceeded to make concise, professional, yet friendly calls every day to request an introductory interview. Each time Greg phoned, he needed to leave a message with Mr. Burk's secretary. She didn't tell him that her boss was out of the town for the next two weeks completing his annual service in the Marine Corps Reserve.

Unlike most of us, Greg didn't give up after the first, second, or third day of silence. He kept calling for eleven days straight. That's right, eleven days! Upon his return, Mr. Burks phoned Greg and said, "I'd like you to come in for an interview. We've never had a management trainee before, but I think it's about time we did."

After Greg and the president of the bank concluded their first meeting, he offered him the job on the spot. "What made you decide to hire me?" Greg felt compelled to ask. "Your professional demeanor," Mr. Burks said, "and most important, your tenacity, son. You called me for eleven days straight about this job. You were like a pit bull with a bone. Of course, I already knew that about you. I have been watching you play college football for four years. I knew you were smart. Now, I also know that you are persistent and focused. People in our community know who you are. I figure we can leverage that with our marketing. It'll be a good thing for all concerned." This is such a valuable lesson. How many of us give up too soon? This kind of perseverance is a critical component of success, provided, of course, it's not *stalking*.

In the beginning, Greg's primary responsibility was to collect back payments on delinquent loans that comprised the savings and loan's portfolio. He would start calling at seven o'clock in the morning until ten o'clock at night, including weekends, and holidays. Within ninety days, Greg's tenacity paid off. The delinquency rate had dropped significantly. After six months, there were only two past-due loans on the books!

In his initial role of management trainee, Greg's salary was $500 per month, which would equate to roughly a hair more than $1,500 today. As his duties shifted to include mortgage origination, Greg's pay scale increased to $1,200 per month plus a $100 car allowance, which was typical compensation during the late '70s, early '80s.

Prior to selling loans on the secondary market, commercial banks and savings and loans funded mortgages with the liquidity derived from new deposits. At Greg's bank, files that had all the supporting documentation were presented to the loan committee every Thursday afternoon for approval. During these sessions, the merits of each package were discussed. The committee looked at the soundness of the collateral as well as the customer's ability to repay. Then they pulled out the balance sheet to determine the amount of reserves they could safely utilize. Loans with the lowest risk were selected to close with the allocated funds. This process remained in effect for most of the five years Greg worked there.

In 1973, Greg's bank began the steps to enter into a relationship with the Federal National Mortgage Association (FNMA). The savings and loan had packaged fourteen loans that met the agency's specifications. Everyone, including Greg, was extremely excited at the prospect of receiving a $1 million check from the sale of their first pool. This was going to be a huge improvement from the way their institution funded loans previously.

However, after several weeks, the money from FNMA had not arrived. The bank's credibility was on the line. Stress levels were high when the president called Greg in to his office. "Greg," he said, "get on a plane, fly to Dallas, and find out what's going on." So off he went, full of confidence, only to be told by the senior underwriter at FNMA, "These files aren't put together properly. You are missing X, Y, and Z. We were just getting ready to ship these loans back to your office." *Really?* This was a surprise. Always quick on his feet, Greg asked if there was any way the underwriter could hold off and let him work from their office to put together the necessary items. After all, how long could it take to get what they needed?

The underwriter agreed. Greg spent the entire day sending and receiving faxes on thermal paper. While he waited for the incoming paperwork, he prepared the necessary documents. On a typewriter! With the forms prepared, and all the required items in his hand, he figured it was time to get the files approved, get his money, and go home. As far as he was concerned, his mission was complete. It made perfect sense to him to ask, "Ma'am, may I please have the check now?" He was told an emphatic, "No. Now that you have provided more complete packages, they will be placed in line to be reviewed." Turn times were running seven to ten days and not a minute sooner. Greg had no choice but to fly home empty handed.

On day seven, Greg called FNMA to check on the status of the payment. He was hoping to hear, "The check is in the mail." Instead, he was told something to the effect of, "What were you and your bank thinking sending us packages that are missing so much critical documentation?" What? He had followed the previous instructions to the letter, or so he thought. Once again, Greg stared at a very long laundry list. He sent the required items via UPS the next day. When another week had passed and the money still had not shown up, Mr. Burks said, "Greg you need to get yourself on a plane, and this time, do not come back without a check. Get FNMA whatever they need. Stay until the job is done."

Once again, Greg flew to Dallas. With steely determination, he went to the offices of FNMA to find out what was still lacking to clear the loans for purchase. The underwriter said, "These packages still aren't put together properly. First of all, they're not stacked in the order of our checklist. Second, not all our required forms are in the file. Third, there are signatures needed on some of the forms you provided. And where are the explanation letters that should be in your files?" Greg had the impression that what she really wanted to ask him was, "Did you and your counterparts just get off the turnip truck?" Greg admits, in retrospect, "She was right. Those first fourteen loans were a mess!"

Once again, he asked if there was a desk where he could sit, and, once again, he was given a place to work. Greg spent the day doing what he had done the last time he was at FNMA—collecting and faxing. Finally, when the files were in the required stacking order, complete with the requested documentation, forms, and signatures, Greg asked, "Ma'am, may I have my check now?"

At this point, one might have expected to hear some epic music playing in the background as Greg collected his money, but, regretfully, that was not the case. Instead, he was told, "You're not getting a check today. Now that you've done your due diligence and have completed the job the way you should have to begin with, our team will put your files in line to be underwritten."

"Ma'am," Greg said, "you don't understand. My boss said I *absolutely* could not leave Dallas until I have a check in my hands. And he means it!"

The senior underwriter finally took pity on him. She reviewed, approved, and cleared the files that very same day. Greg flew home with his million dollars. The next week, he was promoted to Assistant Vice President.

Greg's dogged determination and consistently predictable results began to get noticed. In 1977, when Greg was twenty-eight years old, DeVargas Savings and Loan Bank offered him a position as President and CEO. If he accepted, it would require him to work in Santa Fe, New Mexico. Greg ran the offer past his mentor and boss who gave him his blessing. That's the wonderful thing about true leaders; they love watching others grow and thrive. They don't begrudge or try to hold back the mavericks in their stable; rather, they encourage and support them.

On Greg's first day, he was handed a cease and desist letter, which had arrived several days before. It had been left unopened by the previous management. Greg could see life was not going to be a picnic at the new job, at least not right away.

Rather than being immobilized, he immediately took action. Greg contacted the Federal Home Loan Bank Board (FHLBB), proceeded to set up a meeting, flew to Little Rock, Arkansas, and negotiated an agreement. He agreed to change operation policies and allow the FHLBB to conduct quarterly audits until they felt comfortable that his institution was fiscally sound. An event that happened in short order. By 1979, DeVargas was *the* most profitable savings and loan in its asset category in the state of New Mexico, and rated seventh in the nation. Talk about an accomplishment for one of the industry's youngest savings and loan presidents! He remained with the bank until it was sold in 1984.

RISK TO GROW

Some people blame President Ronald Reagan for the high interest rates of the early 1980s. However, when Greg and I discussed those years, he said "This simply isn't so. It was during Jimmy Carter's presidency that the cost of money began to rise into the teens. Within a couple of years, rates had jumped from 7 percent to as high as 21 percent." In his opinion, "Carter created a situation in which our nation was in a state of inflation while the economy was stagnating. It went beyond all reason and sound economic thinking." Greg as well as leading economists refer to this as "stagflation."

Banks were losing money hand over fist. The need to cut costs was paramount. Somewhere down the line, a group of industry people got together and decided they'd pay loan officers by commission rather than the customary salary plus car allowance. This is how the concept of basis point earnings, or commissions, began, and became the norm.

The early adopters of this policy didn't look past their current reality. The purpose of the change was to save on their fixed costs, which included the expenses associated with paying the loan officer. Imagine what those profit and loss statements would look like today if salespeople were paid as they were before. We may find out; Some feel we're heading in this direction now.

By the mid-1980s, interest rates were steadily decreasing opening the floodgates for refinancing. Originators were making more in earnings than most bank executives including Greg. He realized there was huge earning potential for those who were willing to forgo a steady paycheck and take a risk on themselves. In 1985, Greg made the decision to join Foster Mortgage as a producing branch manager and their Vice President of New Mexico operations.

Commission scales were considerably different at the time Greg started his sales career. The charge to the consumer was a 1 percent origination fee calculated on the amount of the loan. The individual and the company split the fee. In the case of an $88,000 loan amount, the origination fee totaled $880. Of that amount, half, or $440, comprised Greg's commission.

In addition to the 1 percent origination charge, loan officers could earn overage. This tended to happen because of a couple of situations. The first occurred when the salesperson indicated a higher discount point was required than the actual cost to acquire a particular interest rate. It was not uncommon to quote an additional .5 percent (or later, at other compa-nies, even more). Another practice at that time was to hedge the market. If pricing improved, the reduction was not passed along to the customer. In both cases, the income to both the originator and the company increased.

Another justification for overage was when a borrower needed extra counseling due to previous circumstances. In order to get the customer to a place where they qualified for the price range they wanted it would require a lot of additional work, sometimes months, for others, a year or longer. To meet the needs of these clients Greg created the "Don't Give Up Plan" as a solution. His platform was a great way to retain prospects and help them in the process. Rather than charge the borrower a fee up front, they incorporated the 1 percent add-on into the cost of the loan. The customer only paid for the service if they received the tangible benefit of homeownership.

There are loan officers today who think a rate hike into the middle 4–5 percent range is hard to sell. Greg reminds us that there will always be borrowers who need money, no matter what the interest rate. He made a very good living during the early '80s *even* when rates were at 18, 19, 20, and 21.5 percent.

SPREAD THE WORD

By 1989, Greg joined a mastermind group that grew out of a Debra Jones Mortgage Super Stars conference. Each member was required to send one good idea a month to the others. This is when his marketing efforts took on a new dimension.

One month, Greg came up with the idea to "blast fax" his weekly loan statuses, approvals, and closings to his borrowers and the agents on both sides of the transaction. Using the newest and latest technology—the *plain paper* fax machine. Greg asked himself why he should keep the stellar job he and his team were performing a secret? Why positively affect just one person when you can gain recognition from many at the same time? Why indeed? This is when Greg's personal and well-known brand started to form.

Word spread like wild fire, and it was not long before his name dominated the Albuquerque marketplace. When real estate agents or consumers thought about getting a mortgage, Greg Frost's name immediately came to mind, not a brick-and-mortar lending institution. That was what he wanted and, more important, that's exactly what he accomplished. Hence the name of our chapter. When people need a tissue, they typically ask for a Kleenex.

That's because they're thought of as one and the same. This is a perfect analogy for Greg Frost's reputation; when people thought of a mortgage loan, they thought of Greg.

He opened Frost Mortgage, a mortgage-banking firm in 1991. Soon, his team had an 8.5 percent market share in the Albuquerque, New Mexico region. They were responsible for closing one out of the twelve mortgages that originated. Our mutual friend Todd Duncan describes Greg as "the Roger Bannister of the mortgage industry. Roger Bannister was the first man to break the four-minute mile and Greg Frost was the first loan originator to show us that consistent multi-million-dollar month originations were possible."

By 1993, Greg had already topped $80 million in annual personal production. Our earliest discussions, as we all convened by the pool, centered on reinventing the handling of the agent relationship. We wondered what would happen if we gave the deals *to* the real estate agents instead of the other way around. Why follow the current conventional wisdom? Now the agent would be accountable for managing the lead and converting it to a closed sale. This put the originator in the driver's seat, changing the experience to a proactive, instead of a reactive one. Talk about a change in dynamic.

Not long after his return to his home base, Greg was approached by Tom LeMaster. During their meeting Tom shared his concept. He knew it was a good one, but to date he had been unsuccessful in getting the real estate community to see the value. His goal was to have Greg back him and gain momentum in the process.

Tom's program revolved around a local phone number that had access to unlimited extensions. The number, along with an extension, attached as a rider to the "For Sale" sign the agent placed in the front yard. Individuals calling the number heard a pre-recorded message describing the home's attributes. Near the end of each day, the phone system would forward a log, to a fax machine, listing the different callers who had accessed the system. Instead of losing potential clients, agents could follow-up with individuals who had shown an interest in the property that same day.

Greg recognized the brilliance of Tom's idea. He offered to purchase the program; however, he had a non-negotiable caveat. He wanted full exclusivity on all sales generated by mortgage professionals. Tom couldn't believe his good fortune. The two men reached a mutually satisfying agreement. Greg invited Tom to his monthly Success Partner Meeting, a once a month lunch meeting he hosted for his top-tier agents. It was here that Greg announced the launch of their new marketing tool. Tom continued to join the meetings from that point on. He received so much value from Greg's message each month; he felt, he too, could be a success selling real estate. However, before he changed careers, Tom wanted Greg's blessing, and he got it.

Greg's real estate partners fully embraced the strategy of the 800 phone number technology. This was the first time a lender had really helped them gain business. To increase the amount of viable leads Greg had to share, he placed monthly ads in the local *Homes Illustrated* magazine. It started out as full-page ad; however, this simply was not enough space. A second page was required which highlighted, on average, forty-eight listings every month. Eventually, *Homes Illustrated* went out of business, and *Homes and Land* filled the void for several years. Now that print magazines are becoming passé, for the most part, consumers can retrieve the codes through services offered on the Internet, such as Zillow.

SALES BY NUMBER

There reached a point in Tom's career where he didn't have the capacity to service their mutual clients. This was when Greg made the decision to hire Arch Telecom as the provider. Today, at seventy-three years old, Tom's still selling and listing homes. He still refers his client base to Frost Mortgage, which now resides under the Primary Residential Mortgage umbrella, where Greg is the Vice President, of National Training.

Clearly, the plan Tom LeMaster presented to Greg was fully aligned with his philosophy that sales is a numbers game. The more buyers a loan officer speaks with, schedules an appointment with, completes a loan application for, the more loans that will ultimately fund. At his peak, Greg generated 600 potential buyer/borrower leads a month from his call capture system. Here's how the numbers broke down each month:

- 600+ leads.

- 322 prospects spoken to.

- 114 pre-qualification appointments scheduled.

- 68 completed pre-qualification (PQ) or to-be-determined (TBD) property applications.

- 34 approved PQ or TBD property applications.

- 19 prospects who converted to closed loans due to this strategy.

At the time, consumers didn't realize that the technology captured the phone number they dialed from. All they knew, after listening briefly, was that they could find out about the amenities in a home not readily accessible from an exterior view. The message also provided the approximate cost to purchase and anticipated monthly payment. Immediate follow-up was, and remains, critical. Reaching out while the iron is hot always produces better results.

Both Greg's office and the listing agent called the lead. Crossover was a non-issue. In the rare cases when it did occur, Greg reinforced the agent's reputation and ability. The same was true when the situation was reversed.

Here is the script Greg has used successfully throughout his origination career: "You are getting ready to look at houses. This is not the time to go out ill-prepared. Just as you would not go to the grocery store without any money in your wallet, the same applies when you're shopping for a home. It's important to *pre-qualify before you buy.* At your appointment, we help you structure a budget that you can live with. This places you in the position to make an offer on a property with confidence. Here are some current times that are available. Which one works best with your schedule?" The adoption of Tom's system contributed considerably to Greg's bottom line. (Note the figures provided above do not include the income generated from other loan officers who also use this turnkey system.)

Yes, massive lead generation is near and dear to Greg's heart, but this is just one of many concepts he used to reach great success. The same is true for the originators who are under his tutelage. Greg constantly provides them with valuable tools to take their production to *extreme* levels. The 800 number alone provided impressive results, but Greg was able to extract even greater benefits by structuring a well-rounded systematic approach. This is what sets him apart from others. From the time he was a young man in his early twenties, Greg understood his inherent strengths. He has always approached growing business and tackling challenges systematically and numerically. Now five decades later, he continues to refine his craft and build upon his very notable brand. Here are a few more of Greg's secrets to success:

- **Your Business cannot be built on a whim.** He always begins by putting his ideas through a mathematical test. Back in the day, Greg made what he calls a hit list of all the real estate agents he knew, wanted to know, or should know. Then, Greg always completed the homework necessary to determine how many transactions an agent was actually closing. He never guessed or assumed. Next, he very methodically went after them.

- **Break bread together.** For many years, Greg scheduled breakfast and lunch meetings with his professional partners and potential prospects *every* day of *every* week. It was during this time that he would begin to learn how his potential prospects conducted business. If he was interested in furthering the relationship, he scheduled their next meal. If not, he thanked them for their time. For those with whom he already had a solid relationship, Greg looked at the time they spent together as a way of keeping his competitors at bay. He refers to this strategy as *prospecting* and *protecting*.

- **It's just as easy to have an audience of many as one.** To this day, Greg's team holds first-time buyer workshops that consistently attract fourteen to forty attendees every time. These events generate three closings a month on average.

- **It's a numbers game.** To earn the money you want, you'll need to work with your real numbers. First, set your annual earnings goal. Now it's time to take a look at what you've done historically. To arrive at the average commission per file, divide your annual earnings by the number of units you closed in the last calendar year. The second part of this process is to divide your average commission into your new income goal. This formula tells you how many units you have to close to be successful. Let's look at the table below:

HISTORICAL INCOME:		DESIRED INCOME:	
Last Calendar Year:	$187,500.00	Current Year:	$250,000.00
÷ # of Units Closed:	100	÷ Avg. Commission:	$1,875.00
= Avg. Commission:	$1,875.00	= # of Units Needed:	133

Stopping here, however, is premature. The next step is to figure out how many prospects you'll need to get in front of to reach your desired income. As with the first portion of this exercise, you'll work from your actual numbers. Divide the units you closed the previous year by the number of people you spoke to or met with. The sum provides your actual conversion rate. Then divide the future number of units you're striving for by this percentile to find out how many prospects you need to connect with to meet your goal.

HISTORICAL NUMBERS:		FUTURE NUMBERS:	
# of Units Closed:	100	# of Units Needed:	133
÷ # of Prospects:	300	÷ Conversion Rate:	33%
= Conversion Rate:	33%	= # of Prospects Needed:	403

In the above table, the math indicates that one out of three prospects will close their loan. The data indicates a salesperson would need to either increase their prospect pool, improve the percentage of loans that close, or both, to hit the desired income goal.

- ◆ **Pay attention to personal branding.** In the early days, Greg's blast fax idea provided liftoff for him because no one else was marketing that way. Today, his personal branding has extended to corporate training, as well as speaking at numerous industry trade associations. Tony Robbins, Todd Duncan, and Steven Marshall's Mastermind events often feature Greg as a guest speaker, as did Zig Ziglar before he passed.

Math works because it provides an objective measurement based on a person's individual performance. Processes and teams that utilize metrics always have a barometer on which to base improvement, removing the drama and stress often associated with sales. It comes as no surprise, then, that one of Greg's favorite quotes is from Aristotle: "We are what we repeatedly do. Excellence, then, is not an act, but a habit." Certainly, Greg has mastered this philosophy.

DREW McKENZIE

BE THE BALL: CONNECT

Told to and shared by Kathleen

---◆---

There is a force in the universe that makes things happen,
and all you have to do is get in touch with it, stop thinking,
let things happen, be the ball.

—CHEVY CHASE, *CADDYSHACK*

TIMELINE	EMPLOYER	ROLE
During the 2007–2008 Financial Crisis	American Home Mortgage	Retail Loan Officer
Present Employer 2017	Everbank	Branch Manager

IT'S FUNNY HOW things start. A person follows the same rituals, expects the same outcomes, and then *bam!* The unexpected happens. Before you know it, an ordinary day becomes the beginning of something spectacular.

Before my career in mortgage banking, I was a high school teacher dating the school's basketball and baseball coach, who later became my husband. During the season, I would often attend the games to cheer him and his players on. I have always enjoyed the atmosphere at these games, especially the chanting from the crowd (parents and staff mostly) as our team added points to the scoreboard. The adrenaline builds as each quarter or inning comes to completion, and, let's face it, there's nothing like a hard-fought win against a worthy opponent. During one of those games, the team's star player came over to introduce himself and personally thank me for my attendance and support of the team. That was the night I met Drew McKenzie. It was a standout moment.

From that point on, Drew made it a habit to speak with me after every game. I can't say for sure whether I was the first person he acknowledged, the second, or somewhere midway through his rounds. What I can state without equivocation is that it certainly *felt* as though he spoke to me first. That sums up the essence of who he is. Drew knows how to make people feel special. That is his gift; people feel better after they have spent time with him.

Throughout his college years, and since he graduated, Drew has kept in touch with me and my husband, John. Soon after graduating from the University of Scranton in 1990, Sea Land Transport recruited him to work for them. The organization epitomized corporate America. Drew was twenty-two at the time, and though he was soon gaining momentum at the company, he knew something was off. He couldn't quite put his finger on what niggled at him; he just knew the fit was not right.

One night, about a year after Drew graduated, John and I had drinks with him in Boston. As friends often do, we shared current events, reminisced about people we knew in common, and talked about both things that mattered and those that were inconsequential. And when our time together came to an end, our bond was tighter than before. That evening, Drew told us a about his first stab at entrepreneurship.

While in college, he had started a birthday cake business. The idea came to him after he'd seen fellow students who were separated from their families feeling homesick on their special day. He shared his concept with his friend who agreed that Drew was on to something. Later they discussed what they had in mind with his friend's mom, a librarian at the school. She not only had access to students' birthdays, but also could generate reports that sorted by birth date. The report listed the name of the student, the parent's name along with their home mailing address. (It's important to note that at that time, the privacy rules, non-solicitation laws, and opt-in requirements of today did not exist.) Armed with this data, Drew and his friend were ready to get started.

Here's how it worked: two or three weeks before a student's birthday, Drew and his partner would send a note to their parents, offering to bake and deliver a homemade cake to their child. "Of course, we'll sing 'Happy Birthday' in person," they wrote, "and, yes, we'd be glad to convey personal messages." Pure genius! What Drew and his colleague had instinctively figured out was a common pain point to which they provided a solution.

Would families have preferred to celebrate together? Absolutely. It just wasn't always feasible. Classes, exams, and other commitments often prevented the student from making the journey home. And equally just as often, because of work, and other obligations, families couldn't make the trip to the campus. This added personal touch provided happiness to everyone involved. Early recipients referred their program to others, and before long they were making noteworthy money. Drew, in particular, made lifelong connections with a large percentage of the student body *and* their families.

By the time John and I met up with Drew that night in Boston, I'd joined the mortgage industry, as a sales manager for Sears Mortgage. We'd driven into town in our brand-new Lexus. I thought nothing of it, but years later, Drew told me what a huge impression this made on him. Not because we owned that particular car, but because we had the ability to own a car like that.

IN THE EARLY DAYS

Although it was still early in my leadership career, I already knew I wanted to hire someone with the attitude and drive that Drew obviously possessed. Before our evening ended, I planted the seed, and, nearly a year later, in 1993, Drew became a loan officer at the New Jersey branch of Sears Mortgage. He was twenty-three years old.

At Drew's point of entry, interest rates were dropping to single-digit numbers for the first time since the late '70s and early '80s. They went from 12 percent, to 9 percent, down to 8 percent in a relatively short time. Refinance opportunities were at extremely high levels, which was the area in which he was fortunate enough to cut his teeth. Seasoned veterans who were out of capacity to handle their current volume levels handed him their overflow, which gave Drew the chance to learn the process, systems, and industry lingo.

When he started at Sears, Drew knew very little about the details and key aspects of mortgage financing. He considered it mission-critical to align himself with people who had the ability to teach him the lending world. Drew surrounded himself with individuals who had the patience to work with his lack of understanding, and whose counsel he trusted. It wasn't easy in the beginning, but he took the time to dig deep.

Drew told me that his years playing basketball and baseball is where he learned not to be afraid to fail. Sure, there were going to be times when players got beat up along the way, but that's just part of playing the game. Sports taught him that when you're in trouble, keep moving. Don't stagnate. Use your strengths and talents, to make the best decision possible, and then act. Applying these same principles throughout his career has served him well.

While he had only a sophomoric comprehension of the real estate industry that first year, it didn't mean Drew lacked the wherewithal to understand the importance of long-standing relationships. Nor was he immune to the fact that his peers had overlooked the importance of paying attention to the purchase market. Similar to his collegiate days, Drew found a niche and he went after it. Even though the refinance market was hot, it would eventually dry up as it was primarily rate driven. Drew felt purchases would always be his bread and butter, as people would always have the desire to own property. The best way to gain access to potential buyers was through the real estate and builder communities.

Drew invested his as much of his earnings as he could afford advertising in the local newspaper and church bulletins. He joined the North Central Jersey Associate of REALTORS, a membership he continues to maintain today. From the start, he attended many, many open houses, providing him with unfettered access to the agent's undivided attention. It also opened the door for him to connect with the potential buyers who toured the home.

Professional partners and borrowers alike love his personality and his sense of humor. Although he was much younger than most of his competitors, the agents gave him a chance and were over the moon about the amazing service they received. Drew did this by making himself readily accessible to others, taking care of their needs as fast as humanly possible. Attorneys and title companies sent *him* leads and Drew reciprocated in kind. He's consistently appreciative, and never forgets to give thanks to every person who has placed their trust in him.

Prior to 2007–2008, as we mentioned in Greg's chapter it was a very common practice to charge overage. Drew was never a fan of doing this. He did not believe in charging more than necessary to his clients and didn't. Just another reason why he continues to have a successful referral-based business today.

I remember one of his first loans was for a woman who worked for UPS. She was slightly demanding and a bit difficult during her transaction. But Drew handled it all very well, and his gracious attitude won her over. The customer was so happy with her experience that shortly after her loan closed Drew started receiving referrals from many *other* UPS employees. They also felt great about how their transactions were handled, referring him to their co-workers, families, and friends, which created an external sales force that continues to work on his behalf.

In the early part of his career, Drew's client mix had consisted primarily of three types of borrowers: FHA, conforming conventional loan amounts, and high-end customers that sought out jumbo financing. Eventually and intentionally, he chose to focus on the latter. Over the course of his career his clientele includes three NFL athletes, six professional hockey players, and two NBA stars. The agents that represented these high-profile clients were connections that he had met through his friends, and neighbors.

In order to attract the customers that he wanted, Drew believed it was essential to be one of them. He had to live in the same neighborhood, patronize the same establishments, and engage in similar hobbies. So, just a few years into his career, Drew and his beautiful wife, Sharon moved into a very upscale neighborhood. Twenty years ago, they bought the least expensive house, located on the nicest street. Although the couple was clear on where they wanted to live, Drew has always been financially conservative, and Sharon was pregnant with their first daughter. They decided it would be best to rent until they found exactly what they had in mind. They lived in a townhome for two years until they bought their five-bedroom, colonial home. It has been a terrific investment, almost tripling in value.

Drew played golf on great courses, invited by friends, neighbors, and business associates. He frequented trendy restaurants for a quick drink and appetizers. Why? Because those were the places his clients spent time at. He and his family were invited by professional partners and clients to vacation where the rich and famous like to go. He did not overspend. He did not go broke. He did not become a phony. He just made genuine connections with people who enjoyed being with him.

Some might shy away from growing themselves in this manner. However, it wasn't difficult for Drew. He's contagiously confident. Drew knew if he infiltrated the lifestyle of his clients, he would become one of them—hence the name of this chapter. He believed this strategy combined with extraordinary performance would produce the positive results he wanted, and it has.

BUILDING RELATIONSHIPS

Drew positioned himself to earn the right to ask for referrals, *always*. That meant his service levels had to be top notch, and consistently so. It meant he needed to treat others in the same manner he expected to be treated. Drew developed a reputation for being Johnny-on-the-spot. Here are a few examples I remember from our shared past.

I ran a sales meeting following a month when my average originator closed just over $2 million in production. That same month, Drew closed over $11 million. During the meeting, I asked him to tell everyone how he'd accomplished this. I'll always remember what he said: "Call them back. Good news, no news, and/or bad news. It doesn't matter. Call them back and do it quickly. It's not easy, but it has to be done."

One evening later that same month, I happened to be in the office when Drew was meeting with a new customer. I heard him say, "I want to tell you in advance that if my phone rings, I'll take the call. I promise to be as brief as possible. I will do the same for you when your application is being processed."

Later I asked him his thoughts behind this philosophy. Drew said his rationale was simple. "The longer a borrower has to wait to have their questions or concerns to be addressed, the more magnified their worry becomes. By answering their call instead of letting it go to voicemail, I am able to provide the information instantly or ascertain what they need. If more than a few minutes is needed, I provide a time range when they can expect me to call back." Then Drew performed exactly as he said he would, which instilled trust and went a long way to strengthen the bond with the client.

Have you ever heard a colleague say it would be best if their family members or friends work with someone else, because they don't want to risk losing the relationship? Drew never thinks this way. He knows his family and friends are in the best possible hands. There is no one else who would handle their loan with the same dedication and care that he and his team provide. This is evidenced by the number of referrals he receives with consistent regularity.

While Drew's path to success might seem smooth, there have been bumps in the road. As his mortgage career continued, he realized his enjoyment stemmed from personal contact much more than paying attention to the details. Paperwork, the ever-changing guidelines, and compliance regulations just weren't his thing, yet ignorance in these areas was not an option.

I recall two examples of where Drew hit roadblocks in regards to this aspect of his career. The first instance involved a construction loan well over $1 million that was referred from a top real estate agent. The day before Drew completed the application, our company's underwriting guidelines changed regarding how the appraised value was calculated on a newly constructed home.

The underwriter denied the file because it didn't meet the new criteria. So there I sat, at nine o'clock at night, on a conference call with the regional underwriting manager (who was at home), the national underwriting manager (who was in Illinois and working late), and our construction expert (whose office was in California). Drew called me every five minutes from a real estate event to find out if the exception we were requesting was granted. We were successful, but not until a few days later.

The other instance that stands out happened after an early morning call with a client who wanted Drew to secure his rate. The conversation took place during a window of time when the lock department was closed. He promised to take care of his customer's request as soon as they opened. Drew's mistake was that he assumed pricing would remain stable. In this case, it did not. Sure enough, rates flew out the window. Some might consider going into a well-crafted explanation of why they couldn't honor their earlier quote. That was not how Drew chose to handle it. Instead, he made the decision to personally absorb the cost differential. To him, going back to the client was not an option. Drew lost most of his commission on that loan, but he considered this a cost of doing business. And learning. Origination mistakes can be expensive and damaging, but they're nowhere close to the price of losing a lifelong client.

PLAY TO YOUR STRENGTHS—HIRE TO YOUR WEAKNESSES

Drew realized it would be difficult, if not impossible, for him to stay on top of all the paperwork, guidelines, and compliance issues and still do what he loved best—face-to-face selling. He made the determination to hire an assistant to free up his time. Drew composed a list of the functions he wanted to shift to someone else. The first team member he brought on was responsible for three main tasks:

- Chase down the documentation needed to submit a file.

- Put the package together for loan approval.

- Track down any trailing conditions required to receive clear-to-close status.

With his new laser focus on selling, Drew's volume grew exponentially. He was so happy with the results that he didn't stop there. Once his assistant was proficient, Drew hired another associate, which led to the formation of his own team. Each person brought talent and skills sets that complemented the areas in which Drew didn't excel. He continues to use this team-building strategy to this day. Some of his team members have been with him for years—a true testament to his exceptional relationship and leadership skills.

Drew played to his strengths and got help with his weaknesses by hiring the right people. Anyone can work at becoming good enough in a weak area, but it's often a struggle, and not a constructive use of their time. Most definitely, there's merit in having a basic knowledge, but beyond that, it makes sense to hire internally or externally to fill that void. The formation of his team allows Drew to concentrate on generating and closing loans.

LEADERS INSTILL LOYALTY

In 2003, Drew, I, and more than 1,000 of our Washington Mutual co-workers joined American Home Mortgage. We were still at AHM when the mortgage crash was just around the corner in 2007. As the bad news started flowing in and the company faced bankruptcy, Drew was one of the first to reach out to me. The topic of conversation didn't center on when or how he could expect his paycheck, like so many other callers. Instead, his concern was about first, his pipeline—where and when would those loans close and at what price. He needed this information to properly inform his clients, so he could do whatever was necessary to provide a positive experience for all involved. Second, what would happen to me, his friend of more than twenty years? What would I do now? Additionally, he was worried about what would happen to his team? Would a new company see the value in keeping them all together or would they think the risk too great?

The answers to his questions about his team were a definite, "Yes." Drew had a stellar reputation. He had a history of high volumes and, just as critical, these loans had performed well. His percentage of EPDs (early payment defaults) and EPOs (early payoffs) was below the industry average. Drew tapped into his connections with leaders at other companies, as well as colleagues who were working at his competitors.

These were ugly times in the mortgage industry and it was nearly impossible to determine who would be in business the next month, week, or even the following day. Finding a new home became almost a full-time job for Drew and so many others. Simultaneously, he had clients whose needs still had to be met. His influx of referrals hadn't diminished even while he was in this state of uncertainty. Imagine the difficulty of taking care of clients with no sense of security or stability. After some trial and error, Drew ultimately found a new home with Citi Mortgage after American Home closed their doors. Citi seemed the right fit for Drew and his group, and it was, for almost six years. Then he took a job as branch manager at Everbank.

While this was all stressful, as well as time- and energy-consuming, Drew maintained his balance throughout. A rather amazing thing about Drew is that he is *not* a 24/7/365 workaholic. His professional life intertwines with his personal life, but not at the expense of himself or those around him.

He has a very close relationship with his brother and sister. He has a large circle of friends. The man is still in touch with people from grade school! Drew visits friends of friends who are in the hospital when they're ill. Besides attending his friends' anniversary parties, weddings, wakes, and funerals, he does the same for their family members. He still finds the time to play basketball, golf, and vacation annually. And with all that he has going on he *never* misses one of his three daughters' events. He may actually have the most balanced life of anyone I know. I believe that is mainly because Drew never separates family from friends or friends from clients.

A key point to take away from Drew's story is his natural gift of providing an extraordinary experience to others. For him, being a loan officer or branch manager is not a job. It's just another way to connect and stay connected with people he enjoys. Things are not always perfect, of course, but Drew loves what he does. He is grateful *every* time his referral family shares potential customers with him.

When Cindy Douglas spoke with Drew, whom she had never met, she was struck by his ability to observe human nature, his natural desire to affect the lives of others through acts of kindness, and his promise delivery. She was impressed that Drew has not left his life to chance. Instead, he has consistently made clear-cut decisions to build and live the way he wants to.

In summary, Drew has followed the principles he learned during his first stab at being a businessperson, philosophies stemming from the core values he acquired while playing sports. They translate into the following four disciplines:

Discipline #1: Embrace a Successful Work Ethic.

+ Be prompt.
+ Be available.
+ Be fair.
+ Don't hide.

Discipline #2: Choose a company that's a good fit. Remember to ask questions.

+ Is it a mentorship culture?
+ Will they support your efforts?
+ Do they execute?
+ Are their programs a match to your clientele?

Discipline #3: Invest in your business with a concentration on personal exposure.

+ Advertise in the local paper.
+ Advertise in local church bulletins.
+ Join and attend the local association of REALTORS® meetings in the area your real estate agents are located.
+ Attend agent open houses.

Discipline #4: Clearly set and manage client expectations.

◆ Probe to learn exactly what their expectations are, then meet them.

◆ Set the stage, explain, and educate to alter unrealistic expectations.

◆ Fulfill the promises you make.

Drew has built a business that is relationship driven. It works for him because he genuinely cares for people. He's taken it a step further by maximizing his connections. Are you doing the same? If not, what's stopping you? Find out the answer to that question and you'll be well on your way to building a lucrative career that is supported by an external sales force.

RETICULAR ACTIVATOR APPROACH: FOCUSED SALES ACTIVATION

Told to and shared by Cindy

———◆◆———

Focus is more important than intelligence.

—DR. NIDO R. QUBEIN

TIMELINE	EMPLOYER	ROLE
During the 2007–2008 Financial Crisis	JP Morgan Chase	Retail Loan Officer
Present Employer 2017	OnQ Financial	Retail Loan Officer

DAVID JAFFE'S ENTRANCE into the mortgage industry was 100 percent driven by his desire to be in control of his own destiny. After graduating in 1986 from the University of California at Santa Barbara with a degree in psychology, he took four years off to ski, work as a whitewater raft guide, and travel. When David returned, he was ready to settle down and start a career. The book, *What Color Is Your Parachute?*, by Dick Boles, had a profound influence on him. After completing the worksheets provided, the professions suggested were real estate and financial planning. David found both fields interesting, so he began to search for work within the financial sector.

He began the interviewing process in earnest; however, none of the companies he met with trusted him to stick with it. They thought he was a flake and would soon be off traveling again once he had earned enough money. But David kept at it, and in May 1990, Great American Bank, a savings and loan, hired him as a loan officer virtually on the spot. They gave him a $1,500 draw for six months. After that, he would be paid straight commission. David had some concerns about being paid that way, but he figured he would be okay. He was temporarily living rent-free with his parents and had relatively few bills. David was excited at the prospect of his new career; his dad, not so much.

Typically, David's father had been supportive of his decisions. But his dad thought there were other careers that had more earning potential, especially since California had sunk knee-deep into a recession just as his son was entering the lending profession. From what his father could tell (and he was right) there weren't any immediate signs of improvement. Housing values were below what many homeowners owed. New construction sales were weak and would remain that way until the later part of the '90s. The significant reduction in military spending combined with recent cutbacks within the aerospace industry would also play a huge role in the escalating unemployment levels. This was particularly true for Ventura and Los Angeles Counties where David planned to build his business.

MAKING IT RAIN

David was twenty-five years old when he started at Great American, and, as he told me, "clueless" about the state of the company. Unbeknownst to him, the bank was at risk of being taken over by the Resolution Trust Corporation, or RTC. The entity is a government-run asset management company, now part of the Deposit Insurance Fund (DIF). David was effectively the only new loan officer they had. The real estate community, however, was fully aware of the institution's status. He found out much later that the bank had hired him because no one else would sign on with them.

David was motivated and worked extremely hard. Still, producing loans was not easy for him that first six months. In David's words, "it's hard to ask real estate agents for business. It's still tough if I don't have an existing relationship with them." At the end of 1990, he had closed four transactions with an average loan size of $160,000. David wasn't the only originator struggling, in an effort to increase their production, Great American Bank sent David and his colleagues to a Pratt-Duncan Group seminar.

The message David heard repeatedly over the next several days was "If you want to stand out from the crowd, it's essential to do things differently." Making unannounced sales pitches, which is what he'd been doing, didn't set an individual above the competition. The audience was encouraged to break the mold and do things creatively. The Pratt-Duncan Group further drove their point home by emphasizing the importance of doing whatever it took to be fully prepared. It was not enough to show up with a box of donuts and a pile of rate sheets when calling on real estate offices.

The speakers were clear: to have an annuity business, it was essential that the originator see the big picture. Instead of having a narrow mindset that was transaction-based, the audience needed to understand there was more at stake than the one $600,000 deal they were vying for. Rather, the transaction was the vehicle that opened the door to a relationship that had a potential lifetime value of six-figures. Loan officers who exceeded expectations could expect their business to grow exponentially by referrals.

To drive the point home one of the presenters gave this example, "Suppose an agent closed two transactions a month. One of their deals was a listing where they represented the seller on the sale of their home. On the other, they assisted the buyer with their purchase. In this scenario that translates to potentially twelve buyers a year from that individual alone. Multiply that by an additional referral from each borrower, the potential value for that one account could be worth as many as twenty-four deals in a one-year period. Now imagine if that same agent broadcast their satisfaction to others in their office. David could easily visualize the compounding effect.

After he returned from the seminar, David began to build a strategic plan. He realized that with only four closed transactions to his name, he did not have a warm pool of real estate agents to choose from. The first thing he needed to do was change that dynamic. From that point forward, every time he was involved in a purchase transaction, David started to consciously cultivate a relationship with the listing agent. After all, once the transaction closed the seller might need his services, but even if they didn't David saw this as an opportunity to prove himself. In his quest to earn their business he diligently communicated throughout the loan process. At the conclusion of the transaction his assistant, Irma, sent out "Just Closed" postcards. The purpose was to notify agents in the same office and those in the surrounding area that the Jaffe team had closed another loan. There were times this activity generated up to fifteen to twenty mailers a month, creating quite a buzz! This is how David generated momentum in his market place, which in turn helped him in building his agent network.

In September 1991, the RTC shut down Great American Bank. This time, David's job search was much easier, and that same month, he started working for American Residential, a correspondent lender. After seeing the benefits he'd gained at the Pratt-Duncan Group event, David became an avid seminar attendee, taking advantage of anything that helped him sharpen his skills. Later, during another one of Todd Duncan's events he heard a panel of loan officers who produced significantly higher volumes than the industry average talk about the methods they used. One of the panelists mentioned using Act!™, a contact relationship management software (CRM). This product provided a central repository for originators to keep track of all the critical data that affected the financial decisions of the borrower.

David's financial planner mind immediately grabbed onto the idea. He had been previously tracking rates, loan amounts, property addresses, and a few other particulars on a Microsoft® Excel® spreadsheet. However, he wasn't recording any other pertinent information. Borrowers also had life events such as job relocations, ARM adjustment dates, college tuition, and retirement. Reaching out prior to these milestones would be just the thing to take his business to the next level. David liked the systematic approach of putting himself in front of his customers when they could potentially need financing *and* getting there before the competition had a chance to pounce.

This was one of the "aha" moments in David's career. Three years later, he had figured out how to make it rain in buckets. About the same time, Chase Manhattan Bank bought American Residential. David chose to stay with the new company.

It was at Sales Mastery™ that David learned about Front Runner Resources, Inc., in the late '90s. The company produced marketing materials and newsletters specific to mortgage lending. Before, if an originator wanted to produce high quality materials such as these to send to their clientele, they had to take the time to design the pieces themselves or hire someone to do it for them. The tool provided a turnkey solution at a very reasonable price. David didn't procrastinate. He bought the products and began implementing right away.

STRUCTURE, STRUCTURE, STRUCTURE

Fast forwarding to the latter part of 2002, David was well on his way to closing 700+ loans that calendar year. He had a strong team: Irma, his marketing assistant; Linda, whose primary function was to catch anything that was falling through the cracks; a processor, and an administrative assistant. However, David found himself up against a new challenge. His nose had been to the grindstone for almost thirteen years. He was successful, but he had no time for his private life. To remedy this situation, David reached out to his Building Champions™ coach Kate Wilson, whom he'd been working with for three months.

Kate flew out from her Bloomington, Minnesota, office. On her first day there, she spent the majority of her time observing the team, determining where inefficiencies existed. At the end of the day, she and David sat down to review her findings: Action was required to manage the increase of production without burnout. The following day they reviewed what David calls his "Life of Loan" process. With an objective eye, they combed through his written procedures. This document outlined all the critical touch points from the time of introduction through the loan process and long after closing. Kate advised him to think of himself and his team as a business and not just a group of people who originate loans. Next they created an organizational chart, listing out the required staff positions needed to support his process. It was from this coaching that David learned the value of structure.

Before getting into his hiring process, it's important to understand what this mega producer was dealing with. Although one of the largest banks in the country employed David, at that time, not all team members had a computer. On top of that, the computers at the branch weren't part of a network. To combat this situation, David had been having his team create shell packages while the transaction was in process. At the onset, these contained the initial lead sheet and application. Later, the appraisal, Note, Deed of Trust, and the HUD settlement statement were included in the final thinned-down version. Kate recommended that David create a less labor-intensive system.

The organizational chart made it abundantly clear that David had staff deficits to the tune of four to six people. He realized if he wanted to maintain his current volume, his first hire needed to be a clone of himself. Then he would tackle the other staff deficiencies.

Jed Herman, a fellow loan officer, had worked at Countrywide since 1999 and started with Chase in July 2002. David saw that Jed met his high standards. After several discussions, the two men came to an agreement and have been together ever since. When Jed first joined his team, David spent the time necessary to train him to handle the clients the same way he did. Once David was confident that his borrowers and professional partners were going to have the same experience as he delivered, he divided the workload: David took care of the needs of his top echelon and brand-new borrowers, while Jed was responsible for originating the balance of loans that came through David's massive network of clients. Today, the responsibilities have shifted and whoever is available first assists the client.

David's next hire, Cindy, came from an employment agency. Her primary role was to answer the phones and manage David's calendar. Within two years she self-taught herself how to process, and her status was elevated to loan processor. She continues to be an integral part of the Jaffe Team today. Over the next six months, two more clerical and two marketing hires rounded out the team.

TECHNICAL INNOVATION

I entered David's life after Kate introduced us during a break at the 2002 Sales Mastery event. The three of us sat in a small alcove within the vast hallways of the Desert Marriott in Palm Springs, California. We ended up spending thirty minutes together discussing how he was currently using his database.

David and I clicked immediately, probably because we both love Kate. Within a short period, we began working together. Before I went to his branch, Kate and I had a preliminary call about what she and David had determined to be his top priorities:

1. Procure computers for all of his staff.

2. Set up a contract with a technology company.

3. Purchase the additional Act! software licenses needed to supply all of David's team members with access to database management.

4. Design and automate proactive touch points for the employee to reach out to the customer, enhancing their experience. The tasks were assigned in congruence with the individual's expected job duties.

5. Make refinements to the tracking reports he used to run his business.

David took care of the first two items before we got started. With the computers networked, the first order of business for my firm was to get the additional licenses installed on all the individual work stations.

Over the next few months, we refined Act! to meet the needs of the team. As we were about to launch the automation piece, it became clear that the database needed scrubbing. Since David had so many repeat clients, there were multiple contacts for the same borrower. The program was extremely simplistic in those days. It didn't have the ability to add multiple loans to an individual contact record. To overcome this, we added an additional tab with custom fields to use as a placeholder for multiple properties owned by the same borrower. David contracted me to work out of his location. We worked side by side for three weeks clearing out the duplicate records. We then created a report that reflected which records were missing an e-mail address or had any other pertinent contact fields that required updating. David and Jed proceeded to reach out to their clientele over the next month until they had completed the job to their satisfaction. The now-scoured database was ready. The automation piece was launched.

David has since outgrown Act! as his primary contact management system, but he still retains the software because it has data stored from the early 1990s. His current company, OnQ Financial, Inc., where he started working in 2009, uses Encompass™ to manage the loan pipeline. David says, the program has excellent reporting capabilities, negating the need for the custom reports we had built into Act! and Microsoft® Excel® years earlier.

Never one to sit on his laurels, David has evolved his method of communication. He now uses BombBomb,™ a video-based e-mail platform to mass market. The Jaffe Team also uses Slydial™ to connect directly to the recipient's voicemail. This works exceptionally well when transmitting information that does not require a return phone call, such as status.

One reason David's customers are so loyal to him is his commitment to consistently monitor their existing rate, which, he has done for twenty-seven years, like clockwork. For the first twenty years, David pulled the report manually on a daily basis at the start of his work day. It told him which clients would benefit from refinancing their existing rate. Now, his pricing engine, Optimal Blue,™ alerts him to these opportunities. Monitoring the rate is not in lieu of reviews he performs annually with his customers, rather it is an extension of the services he offers. David still tracks birthdays and financial goals too. He is religious about reaching out and staying in touch.

Still, even with all the process improvements, he has in place, and his excellent team, David's production temporarily suffered in the latter part of 2007 and into the financial crisis of 2008. However, the mass exodus of originators within his demographic led to a reduction in competition. This in combination with the drop in interest rates caused his production to pick back up in 2009. That year, the *Scotsman Guide,* David ranked #17 in the country for dollar volume at $143,019,795. He closed 390 units, which put him at #42 for the most closed loans in the country. Since then, being in the top 100 nationally is the status quo for David, a ranking he has achieved every year for over the last eighteen years.

YEAR	RANKING	DOLLAR VOLUME	CLOSED UNITS
2016	81	$152,559,130	341
2015	53	$145,051,821	337
2014	52	$104,096,571	254
2013	29	$147,568,913	413
2012	9	$224,382,737	606
2011	18	$154,169,282	412
2010	9	$188,106,724	493

In 2009, JPMorgan Chase purchased Washington Mutual Bank (WaMu), causing Chase to change their home loan model. Unlike WaMu, Chase didn't have bank branches on the West Coast. Prior to the acquisition, offices similar to the one David worked out of were stand-alone mortgage offices that were 100 percent responsible for self-sourcing business. However, once the purchase was completed, Chase placed many of their originators in the newly acquired branch locations. Instead of loan officers going out and getting business, the new model had them sitting in the bank, at their desk waiting for the phone to ring. This philosophy would support increasing the branch's bottom line by reducing the commissions paid to the originator since they didn't self-generate the lead. It would also jeopardize David's ability to provide the same stellar service for his long-term clients and referral partners. These were relationships he had spent his entire career cultivating.

On top of this, the conditioning on loan files was, in David's words, "craziness." Ninety days became the norm to close most refinances. It was nearly impossible to meet the deadlines stated in the purchase contract. Because of this, he arrived at the difficult decision to leave Chase. His preference was to work for a correspondent lender, but it seemed they were all going out of business or losing their warehouse lines of credit. David was afraid he would have to change companies again if he went in that direction, so instead, in June 2009; he accepted employment with Bank of America. Ninety days in to it though, David realized the culture wasn't right for him. It took him almost another three months to find a new job. Near the end of 2009, he accepted a position with OnQ Financial, a correspondent lender.

By 2014, in spite of all the systems he had created and was using, David felt so burnt out that when a referral called in to inquiry about a purchase or refinance, he felt a wave of anger at being interrupted. He didn't want to talk to anyone, and was seriously considering retiring. However, every time he thought about walking away, he just couldn't do it. He had twenty-seven years of blood, sweat, and tears invested in what he'd built. After talking with his friend, Jeff Lake, David did some soul searching. He decided he could restructure the business, cut his hours, *and* still earn enough income to support his present lifestyle. What it boiled down to was that David needed to hire some additional help.

Once again, David found the perfect fit right in his own organization. Holly St. Germain had been the Sales Integration Manager for OnQ when David started there. She'd since been promoted to Vice President, California Sales Manager with responsibilities that included being in charge of recruiting and management for the entire state. David felt she did an amazing job. He thought her skill sets would really complement his team. Holly didn't have an ounce of call reluctance, so she has attracted many new agent relationships, adding constant value to the Jaffe Team. Bringing Holly on as his senior mortgage consultant has completely reinvigorated David, giving him new energy to continue with his career. He has reduced his hours from fifty-five to thirty per week allowing him to give back by mentoring other loan officers. He has also become more involved in charitable work—things that he has wanted to do for a very long time.

TEAM WORK

Team Jaffe has refined its business model throughout the years, really upping the "Life of Loan" process David developed—a system based on Ken Blanchard's "Raving Fans" philosophy. Listing agents still receive a welcome call from David, Jed, and Holly depending on who is assisting the borrower with their financing. Predefined e-mail templates notify all parties once critical milestones happen, including the date the file is submitted to underwriting, receipt of the appraisal, the issuance of final documents, and loan closing. Delivery of weekly status occurs via a live phone call every Tuesday.

The final loan package sent to the closing agent contains a survey for the customer to complete at funding. With permission, the comments serve as testimonials. The Jaffe team also conducts a mid-process review with the borrower to make sure they are feeling good about their experience. While customers appreciate the care received during the transaction, what keeps them coming back is David's tremendous follow-up after closing. It starts with the Closed Loan booklet that the team provides for the client's records. It contains a copy of the appraisal, Closing Disclosure, Note, and Deed of Trust. And as mentioned throughout this chapter, David is a big proponent of database management, attributing it as one of the major factors that has contributed to the success he has enjoyed. To refresh, here are some of the times the team reaches out to their clientele:

- ◆ ARM rate adjustments.

- ◆ Loan closing anniversaries.

- ◆ Birthdays.

- ◆ Who I Helped postcards.

- ◆ Client events, such as renting out a movie theatre.

These are intentional calls that David, Jed, and Holly make to the people in their database; they are not preprogrammed correspondence. Although there are other materials sent consistently, such as the newsletters mentioned earlier, it's these calls that set them apart from their competition. All three have specified time blocks in their calendars to complete this function daily. It's that important. To this day, most of David's business is a result of his continual contact with his database of closed clients. They might be looking to move-up, scale down, refinance, or send a referral his way. The balance, or about 35 percent of his transactions, are referrals from his real estate partners. David expects this ratio will even out now that Holly has joined the team.

Outside of work, David enjoys family time with his wife and two children. He is an avid traveler and especially enjoys the tropics. He is also an active supporter of Project Understanding, Casa Pacifica, and other organizations in Ventura County. He continues to educate himself by attending industry events and reading books that involve psychology.

Bonus:

Reticular Activator Marketing!

by David Jaffe

"Do you know about your reticular activator?" Reticular means screen-like or filter-like. It also refers to the very deep part of your skin. Your reticular *activator* is the part of your brain that helps you sort out the things that are important to you from the ones that are not; it is specifically the *alert* part. With all the information that inundates you, something has to help you filter it, so you can concentrate on what is important. That is the reticular activator!

For example, suppose you are walking down the concourse at the airport, oblivious to the dozens of announcements made over the loud speaker. Suddenly, you hear, "David Jaffe, pick up the white courtesy phone." That catches your attention! The fact that you heard your name but none of the others is proof positive that your reticular activator is working.

For me, it is also about little children. Before my son was born, I rarely noticed little kids. Now, everywhere I go, I see preschoolers and toddlers just learning how to walk, talk, and interact. That is what is important to me.

In real estate financing, you have dozens of conversations with people about mortgages. All the Jaffe Team's business comes from referrals of current and past clients. Our team is fond of saying, "I know you're going to like working with us and the way we do business, just like the person who referred you to us."

The Jaffe team constantly tries to establish themselves as a client's reticular activator. In turn, they always keep their clients in *their* reticular activator. Then the team follows up so the client's reticular activator always thinks, *Mortgage—Jaffe Team. Friends and family mortgages—Jaffe Team.*

DON'T FAKE IT UNTIL YOU MAKE IT: JUST DO IT RIGHT

Told to and shared by Cindy and Kathleen

————————◆※◆————————

The secret of your success is determined by your daily agenda.

—JOHN C. MAXWELL

TIMELINE	EMPLOYER	ROLE
During the 2007–2008 Financial Crisis	American Home Mortgage	Executive VP
Present Employer 2017	Guaranteed Rate	Regional Manager

NOT ONLY HAS Jeff Lake succeeded in gigantic measure, he *loves* what he does. Imagine that. Jeff has always paid attention to what his clients ask for, and then he delivers on that request. He believes this is what gives the Lake Team its edge over the competition. In Jeff's words, "If the client asks for chocolate, then give them chocolate. Stop pushing toffee. Our approach is a combination of Nordstrom's and Walmart's philosophies. We give great service at everyday low prices. When our clients go to the loan closing, they receive what they expect every time. We make certain there are no surprises, disappointments, or unmet expectations."

Throughout this chapter, there will be several examples of how Jeff observes opportunity where others do not. Then, what's even more critical, he acts. Let's look at how this entrepreneur created a saleable business-within-a-business by putting systems in place, systems that his team could follow whether he was physically present or not. When Jeff chooses to step down completely he will hand over the reins to his team. The model he created will serve as a legacy to them, a reward for the loyalty they've shown throughout the years.

Jeff's definition of customer service was formed early on from observing how his father ran his restaurant supply business. Often his dad received calls from his customers over the weekend when they ran out of inventory. When that happened, he loaded up the back of his truck with the requested items making sure the deliveries happened on time. The fact that his father understood and appreciated the urgency made him an invaluable resource. This left a lasting impression on Jeff. So much so that these became his core convictions:

- Treat people with respect. It's about how *they* want to be treated; not how *you* want to be treated.

- Beat the client's expectations, don't just meet them.

- Always look out for the best long-term interest of the client, and all parties concerned. This includes watching out for your own business with just as much care.

SHIFTING GEARS

In 1977, in a very different time, before the mortgage business was on Jeff's radar, he and his brother-in-law formed a company that promoted concerts in Arizona. They also owned nine retail music shops. Those were wild times. The classic rock-n-roll way of life was filled with flash, groupies, parties, and every recreational drug imaginable. It was tough to stay within the boundary lines. Musicians knew how to have fun, and so did Jeff; lots of fun.

Jeff eventually recognized he was in a downward spiral. The year was 1985. His marriage had suffered past the point of saving. The decision to break ties was mutual. He parted ways with his wife, signed everything over to his brother-in-law and partner, and never looked back. Later, when his mortgage practice started sucking up all of his free time, Jeff would reflect on his time in the music business as a reminder of what *not* to do.

In 1986, recently divorced, with $600 in his pocket, Jeff moved back to Chicago, living with his mom and dad until he could reestablish himself. His brother owned Old Republic Title and put him to work as a title representative. His sole job was to target mortgage offices. As long as he met the minimum sales quota, he would be paid $700 per week. Jeff had no problem meeting this criterion. It did not take long before he realized there was a boatload of money to be made in mortgages. Most people needed or preferred to borrow the funds required to purchase a home. Based on his initial impressions of the loan officers he was calling on, most just waited for the phone to ring. Jeff knew he could leave them in the dust, *and* he did.

In October 1986, he landed his first mortgage gig. It was with Cityfed Mortgage Company, a national lender based in Puyallup, Washington. They had a branch in the Chicago metro area, which is where Jeff called home. His training consisted of riding shotgun with a couple of older, jaded gentlemen for a few days to get the lay of the land. Their attempt to teach him the business was more like the sharing of war stories. Each tried to best the other. Afterward, his boss handed him a rate sheet and said, "Don't come back until you have a loan to bring me." Jeff thought, *Okay,* and did exactly that. He fell into one within his first two or three weeks.

His second deal came from a new real estate agent, Linda Goland, who'd been with Coldwell Banker for six months. Jeff was surprised to receive this opportunity from her. She had a first-time homebuyer who worked at Sears. Come to find out, the only reason he got the deal was because Sears didn't have the program the borrower needed. Cityfed, where Jeff worked, featured a product called the one-year Growing Equity Mortgage™ (GEM), also known as a Sure Step loan. What made his product special was that it only required a 3.5 percent down payment versus the typical 20 percent associated with the conventional financing offered at Sears.

The Cityfed GEM loan was a terrific option for borrowers whose income was going to steadily increase over the next few years. The monthly payments rose over time according to a set schedule. Borrowers were able to pay off the principal balance at a faster rate than a standard thirty-year mortgage. This fixed rate loan was fully amortized. Linda's client didn't want to cough up the 20 percent down, but he liked the idea of paying off sooner.

She watched Jeff like a hawk; reaching out to him constantly. She warned Jeff of the damage his reputation would suffer if this loan didn't close on time. He wasn't worried in the least. Jeff knew he would close the loan on time, and he did. Today, Linda continues to be one of his advocates.

Within nine months of starting his origination career, Jeff was the fourth highest producer for his company. This earned him the status of "Rookie of the Year." He closed $13 million in volume, which translated to a six-figure income that year, with an average loan size of $100,000! It was not long before other companies began to solicit Jeff in earnest to come work for them.

One of the interviews Jeff had was with a local mortgage broker. He indicated that Jeff would have the ability to make a lot more money if he came to work for him at his brokerage. Since Jeff's role would be that of a customer instead of an employee, lenders would cater to him. In short, this would mean faster turn times and reduced loan conditions, resulting in more deals. It is worth noting that Jeff was not looking to leave his current position. Based on what he heard, however, the move made sense. Though it sounded rosy on the surface, the reality turned out to be a different story. The person who owned the brokerage never paid him. Eventually, Jeff won a judgment for the money that was owed to him, but it was too little, too late; his boss didn't have the funds to pay him.

NO SUCH THING AS LUCK: PREPARATION MEETS OPPORTUNITY

Jeff's main source of business came from real estate agents. To create the perception of demand he held the bulk of his borrower appointments in the agent's office. Jeff made sure to show up fifteen to thirty minutes early. That gave the other sales agents a chance to ask him to pre-qualify their customers when *he* had the time. Intrinsically, Jeff knew the agents associated his presence with success. If someone else in the office trusted their livelihood with him, then they could too.

Jeff was creating social proof in person instead of online. He was constantly putting himself out there, enabling salespeople to see him. Jeff spent his weekends at open houses. He chose homes that had great street appeal because they had a better chance of increased foot traffic. Since his competition did not take the same initiative, Jeff had the first shot with prospective buyers that stopped by. He also had the full attention of the agent when there was a lull in the action.

As we've seen again and again, Jeff leaves nothing to chance. He creates opportunity whenever he can. If Jeff wasn't at an open house or calling on real estate offices, he was attending a variety of functions at the North Shore and Northwest Association of REALTORS, including dinners, meetings, and caravans. Later, these two associations would combine with the Chicago Association of REALTORS. Jeff wanted to make sure he was seen and heard at *all times*. He networked with everyone, including fellow affiliate members. It was here Jeff often had conversations with mover and shaker, John Manglardi, the owner of Century 21 Northwest Realty.

It did not take John long to realize there was more to Jeff than his easygoing personality. Appreciating Jeff's brilliance, charisma, and rainmaking ability, John actively courted him. He wanted to incorporate Jeff's innate talents into the mortgage company he planned to open. After a year of discussion, and his initial investment of $47,000 to buy-in, First Home Mortgage was born in 1987. Jeff filled the sales manager role, John handled the financial end, and another individual was brought on in 1991 to manage operations.

First Home was wildly successful. By 1989, Jeff was juggling the responsibilities of running a company, attending numerous meetings, and originating loans. He was never home. Every minute of his day was filled to capacity, and then some. Jeff had remarried the year before. He wanted to spend more time his wife, Shari, and their one-year-old daughter, Ashley. As a single person, being consumed by work hadn't been a problem, but now, it was. Thinking the issue with his long work hours was how he managed his time, Jeff invested in coaching and attended seminars, but it didn't help.

Looking back, Jeff realized that the crux of the problem was not what he believed it to be. He was in fact an efficient scheduler. The issue was in how he chose to allocate his time. Instead of capitalizing on his existing relationships, he was devoting 75 percent of his time chasing new deals. That changed when all the pieces fell into place.

First Nationwide Bank invited Jeff and his team to a three-day event where there would be several high-end trainers. He brought twenty of his salespeople. The entire group totaled several hundred people. One of the featured speakers began her session by having everyone stand up. She asked those in the audience who had closed $10 million in volume or more the preceding year to remain standing; the rest were to sit down. She raised the bar to $20, $30, and then $40 million. As the number grew higher, the group became significantly smaller, until Jeff was the only one left standing.

At the end of the third day, the presenter asked if Jeff would join her for lunch, which he later did. She told him about her associate, Todd Duncan, who interviewed top producing originators for his audio series. As part of their annual subscription, subscribers received a new tape each month. Interviewees received copies to use as a recruiting tool. When asked if he wanted to participate, Jeff said he did.

After Todd conducted the interview with Jeff, he was so impressed that he invited him to his Achieving Leadership Excellence," or ALE, conference held in Lanai, Hawaii. The participants at the 1993 summer retreat agreed to form a mastermind group. They would meet monthly, mostly by phone, but other times in person to brainstorm and share ideas. Todd considered these twelve individuals to be the brightest minds in the mortgage industry at that time.

Jeff arrived at two conclusions on the trip. One, he needed to build a team that served him. This would allow him to delegate tasks that did not require his expertise or intervention. Two, he needed to compound the fruits of his labor by building and nurturing relationships that mattered to him.

THERE ARE ENOUGH PEOPLE WHO WANT TO DO BUSINESS YOUR WAY

Jeff attributes the second conclusion he reached for having the greatest impact on how he conducted future business. Todd's message was loud and clear: "There are enough people who want to do business your way. Get rid of the rest." Jeff agreed wholeheartedly. He was tired of chasing agents. It was time to get more business from the customers he had instead of trying to work with everyone and anyone.

This change in direction led to Jeff's annual volume increasing from $60 million to $300 million at the height of his career. While his production was on the rise, his average workweek went from seventy-plus to fifty hours a week. That's a reduction of almost 30 percent. After that first ALE session, Jeff *never* worked another Sunday again. Later he reduced his hours even more as his team took over running the business. Today, Jeff lives in Arizona full-time and visits his Chicago location three to four days a month. That's right, *and* he still earns a *very* lucrative income from the enterprise he's built. July and August are the exception, however, because the influx of business during both months is significantly higher than the rest of the year.

His first plan of attack was to develop a two-page questionnaire that would help him delineate which agents fit his criteria. It began:

- How long have you been in business?

- What are your annual sales?

- How many buyers do you work with?

- What are your sales projections for the remainder of the year?

Most of the thirty agents Jeff invited to his office stopped halfway through filling out the first portion. They wanted to know why he was asking them those questions. Jeff's reply was the same each time: "How do you know where your business is going if you don't know your numbers? Life is too short to be working all the time. Think about how much time you waste driving around in a car showing houses to prospects that never go anywhere. It's critical to quantify your business. That's why this exercise is important to you. There's more to life than work; by working smart, you'll have more time to enjoy it."

In his quest to find people who were willing to do business his way, Jeff wanted to put things in perspective for the agents who accepted his invitation. He pointed out that on a $300,000 deal they earned 3 percent or $9,000. However, his commission was .5 percent or $1,500. Jeff knew he worked equally hard, yet the earnings were unbalanced. He told each one, "I have made the decision to improve my quality of life. Making money is great, but not at my family's or my expense. That means having partnerships with professionals who see the value in the way I work and are willing to send every potential deal they come across my way." To even the playing field, Jeff expected them to increase the number of deals they'd been sending to him. He was going to have a better lifestyle and he wasn't interested in working with those that did not concur with his way of thinking. In the end, 50 percent, or fifteen of them, who met with Jeff agreed to his terms. Those who didn't, he cut loose.

Jeff had shifted his mindset regarding the real estate professionals on his team. Instead of thinking about them as his clients, he began to consider them his business partners. This led him to create a contract that would specifically state each parties' responsibilities. The agents agreed not to discuss rate, fees, or loan terms with the referred consumer. In turn, Jeff reciprocated by not discussing the location or anything that had to do with the property itself.

Why would someone sign this contract? Simple. Those who held up their end of the bargain received qualified customers from Jeff. It's important to note that the referrals he provided were fully vetted, capable, and motivated buyers and sellers. This meant less time wasted on looky loos who just needed to kill time on a Saturday or Sunday afternoon. It also provided an extra level of safety for his female agents. Jeff's plan was in the best interest of all concerned.

One of his agents was the top RE/MAX agent in Illinois. She was generating all kinds of business through the implementation of an 800-number strategy. The provider, Arch Telecom, offered a toll-free number with individual extensions. Greg Frost used this same vendor after Tom LeMaster started selling real estate full-time. Jeff's agent had three to four telemarketers following up on these leads, but the stream was so intense that they couldn't get back to callers quickly enough. She asked Jeff if he had any interest in participating in the lead follow-up. Naturally, he did; this was another source of generating business.

To mitigate the risk of his business dropping off due to outside forces such as the economy and market conditions, he decided to expand his pillars of business. If one segment was tanking, it made sense to have another sector that was doing well. This would help insulate Jeff from the potential for peaks and valleys that are common in the lending industry. While he was coordinating his efforts with his real estate partners, he got busy building other potential income streams.

THE GOLD ADVANTAGE

Computer Discount Warehouse, also known as CDW, became Jeff's first corporate account. When Jeff met the founder through his wife's best friend, it was at the right time—the owner wanted to take CDW public. That meant he needed momentum. Jeff knew he could create a program that would provide the traction the owner sought. The premise behind Jeff's platform was simple: reward loyalty.

Instead of reinventing the wheel, Jeff emulated the core tenets that American Express had successfully incorporated with their Premier Rewards Gold Card. Employees who were in good standing at CDW received a Gold Advantage card. This piece of gold plastic looked and felt like an elite charge card. Employees presented the card at local retailers to receive significant discounts. It was impressive. Customers in line would want to know how they could get one. Although the cards were not created to act as mini billboards, in the end, that's exactly what they ended up being. This was one of the benefits CDW and future employers under Jeff's program received.

At one of the mastermind sessions he attended, Jeff talked about the leads he was getting from his agent who was using the 800 number technology and his corporate marketing strategy. He shared that one of the problems he was running in to was finding an effective way to increase retention. His colleague Greg Frost, who was in the same group, indicated he had a solution to deal with that exact challenge. He shared his Don't Give Up Plan and explained how it was geared specifically toward people who needed some time to get their affairs in order to qualify for a home loan. Jeff really liked the concept and asked for Greg's approval to incorporate the plan into his own model.

With Greg's blessing, Jeff and his partner adapted the Don't Give Up Plan. The CDW employees were already reaching out to the Lake Team via a wall-mounted red phone that he had installed in the break room—red to imply urgency. Its entire purpose was to give individuals an opportunity to call-in to request a free credit report. During the conversation, they found out what it would take to qualify for a home loan or refinance an existing one. Workers who had credit challenges were set up on the new program.

Nearly 20 percent of those with credit issues were motivated to participate. Then, when they were in a position to qualify for a mortgage, they were eligible to receive the same reduction in loan fees and real estate commissions as their peers. Regardless, even those with credit challenges were eligible for the Gold Advantage card. Eventually, Kraft Foods Group, Allstate, Underwriters Laboratory, Motorola, and Abbot Laboratories adopted Jeff's Gold Advantage program.

CUSTOMER CONNECTION

Jeff knew the platform he created was off to a great start, but he also needed to do more to further his retention efforts. He decided to create a monthly newsletter that he called *The Advisor*. Jeff hired a ghostwriter to assist him. The publication went out monthly, keeping him front and center so his current and potential clients wouldn't forget him.

Attorneys were another one of Jeff's resources, particularly divorce attorneys. He liked this avenue of business because there was often the possibility to get two or more transactions. Besides needing to sell their property, many times both parties often turned around and purchased another home. There were instances where they needed to liquidate multiple properties. Lawyers who represented bankruptcy clients also had referrals.

Jeff also instituted a mastermind breakfast that he opened to agents of his choosing. He brought in high-caliber guest speakers, such as economists, and others who offered insight about current and future market conditions. In the beginning, the newly formed group found it difficult to openly share. Many said, "I can't do this." Jeff's reply was always, "Yes, you can." The groups' reluctance stemmed from their natural tendency to be territorial. They feared giving up their competitive edge. However, it didn't take long before they realized that the business value Jeff brought to the table far outweighed their concerns. In addition, members were encouraged to refer amongst themselves any clients who weren't in their geographic purview.

Jeff began conducting client surveys. He had his loan opener call all customers within seven to ten days after their transaction closed. This gave homeowners a chance to settle in. The opener said that she was a member of the quality control department at First Home. She asked what the team could do to improve their service levels. In addition, she also found out who referred Jeff to them, and the name of the agent who had assisted with their purchase.

Her primary objectives were first, to determine ways to improve the loan process for future transactions. And second, and just as important to Jeff, to provide a realistic picture of which agents had the most influence with their mutual clientele. Half the callers couldn't even remember who their agent was. Considering such a short time had passed since closing, this was a sad state of affairs. At the conclusion of every call, his employee always said, "Please don't keep Jeff a secret. Is there anyone you know who could use his services?" Immediately 10 percent always had a new prospect to recommend. That equated to more than one hundred loans a year!

After reviewing the responses, Jeff contacted the agent who'd represented the buyer and shared the results of the post-closing survey. For those agents whose customers hadn't remembered their name, Jeff ended their conversation with a few words of advice: "You should call these people because they don't really know who you are. How can they refer future business to you? If you let them slip away you're leaving money on the table and handing it over to your competitors on a silver platter."

With all this tracking and customer focus, Jeff needed a better tool than Microsoft® Excel® to stay on top of everything. His use of contact management became even more intentional when he started using Mortgage Quest¨, a software customized specifically for the loan professional. The program had much of the same ability as the Act!™ program used by David Jaffe. It had a place to enter notes, keep a log of conversations, store critical information about the borrower's loan, and record personal milestones. It also had a calendar feature. Since the CRM was housed on the network Jeff's entire team had full access and knowledge of the client, providing an even better customer experience. Eventually the Lake Team switched over to Goldmine¨.

Instead of having to spend hours scouring his Microsoft Excel workbook, Jeff used the calendar view to see a list of potential high-dollar-producing activities. He delegated a number of these tasks to one of the three loan officers he had working for him. These knowledgeable individuals were fully capable of handling the transaction from start to finish. They just didn't have the rainmaker skills Jeff possessed. It was a win-win for all concerned.

BUILD YOUR OWN BUSINESS

In 1995, the company's closed loan volume reached $100 million. Jeff's contribution was 60 percent, or $60 million! By 1999, First Home had grown to closing $2 billion a year in production. The company was too big to be considered small, yet too small to be considered big. Getting credit lines was becoming more difficult for an entity of their size.

In the same year, the CEO and founder of American Home Mortgage approached Jeff and his two partners to discuss joining his startup company. The firm's corporate office was based out of Melville, New York. The three men were definitely intrigued. Jeff realized that signing on with AHM would give him the opportunity to be a decision-maker in an organization with huge expansion possibilities. What really appealed to him was the idea that he would not need to be involved in the running of the day-to-day operations. First Home merged with AHM February 2001.

The Lake Team soared to new heights as Jeff concentrated all his efforts on loan origination. In April 2002, *Mortgage Originator* magazine recognized Jeff as the top-producing mortgage consultant in Illinois for the eleventh consecutive year. For ten years in a row, Jeff ranked among the top ten loan originators in the nation. By 2004, Jeff, Shari, and daughter, Ashely were dividing their time between their Chicago residence and their ranch-style home in Tucson, Arizona. Life was good, very good.

2005 was the year Jeff developed a mentorship program for loan originators called Mortgage Solutions for Generations.™ Managers recommended sales staff who met the production and income standards Jeff had in place. Candidates attended a two-day boot camp known as Build Your Own Business, or BYOB. The event was held in two locations, Chicago and Tucson. The first day was spent giving a general overview of what the six-month mentorship program involved. Loan officers who wanted to participate and who were accepted into the program agreed to pledge $5,000 from their earnings. They were only expected to pay this fee if they didn't complete the required course work. Those who did stay on task throughout the term were rewarded two-fold. The fee was waived in its entirety and they earned an additional fifteen basis points on every loan they closed for six months after they graduated. The Loan Officer Compensation Rule was not in place until several years later, which meant this was a significant increase in pay.

Day two was a more extensive overview of what was expected of participants. It was explained that individuals would need to dedicate a significant amount of time to complete the assignments. The curriculum included weekly group calls as well as individual biweekly accountability sessions with Jeff. For this program to be of value, participants *had* to be truly invested in their futures. Nearly 40 percent didn't finish. Either they made the decision to leave on their own or the decision was made for them. Those who didn't hang in there were required to pay back the pledged funds. The payment was negotiated with the manager who recommended them. In 2016, Jeff signed the service mark for Mortgage Solutions for Generations over to his team lead, Jo Ann.

As with other programs and solutions Jeff had implemented, he was way ahead of his time. He received immense satisfaction from his involvement with BYOB. It is also partially how American Home Mortgage grew some of the industry's top loan originators. Here are what two graduates had to say about Jeff:

"I never knew Jeff was an executive Vice President. Why? Because Jeff was not a manager. He was not a boss. Jeff was a Leader. Leaders do not need titles; they lead and people follow. Jeff led by example. Jeff also taught. I had the pleasure of being coached by Jeff in 2006 and to this day, once a month, I review my notes from our coaching sessions. I am still finding things I can implement. It was a pleasure to work with and to be taught by the #1 loan officer . . . ever. Thanks, Jeff."—Julie Miller

"I have had the privilege to work with Jeff as my business coach. He is the foundation of much of what I practice in my business today. Jeff is very thorough, with proven strategies for success that apply whether you are in mortgage or any other business. Personal touch and consistent follow-through. Jeff teaches what he practices. He is one of the most successful mortgage professionals in his field, and I'm privileged to be coached by him." —Deanna Valeo

It is worth noting that both these mortgage professionals continue to enjoy huge success in the industry today.

Jeff was making a big difference. By 2007, things were going great . . . until they were not. He saw the writing on the wall about thirty days before American Home closed their doors that August. Once AHM made the formal announcement, Jeff immediately picked up the phone and called every one of his clients. He didn't want them finding out when they watched the evening news. He packed up roughly *fifty-plus* physical loan packages and literally placed them into grocery cartons. Then he went to work. He reached out to every possible outlet he knew of that could possibly get these deals closed. Jeff didn't make a dime on those loans, and in the present state of affairs, he didn't care. His primary concern was not for himself, but for the welfare of his clients.

Jeff's phone was ringing off the hook. Headhunters were hounding him to come work for the mortgage companies they represented. One of the calls he received came from Guaranteed Rate. When the founder and CEO, found out that his recruiter had called Jeff, he picked up the phone and left a very warm message on his voicemail. He expressed that if there was anything he could do to help him, all he had to do was ask.

Prior to receiving his message Jeff managed to get the majority of his pipeline closed with the other companies he had reached out to. However, he still had eight non-conforming (jumbo) loans that were submitted as interest only, adjustable rate mortgages. They had closing deadlines in the next two days. Thornburg, a correspondent lender was the only outlet at that time that offered this particular product. The packages had been fully underwritten and were cleared to have the final papers drawn.

The challenge was that Thornburg wasn't comfortable closing these deals with other lenders. Their relationship had been with American Home. Jeff decided to reach out to Guaranteed's CEO and take him up on his offer to help. They agreed to meet the following day at nine o'clock in the morning.

While the two men were meeting, Guaranteed's underwriters reviewed the files. Six of the eight loans were blessed immediately. The CEO committed to closing those on the spot. Of the two loans that were in question, one was easily rectified. Changing the term from a 3/1 to a 5/1 ARM made all the difference. The market had improved, making the loan more saleable on the secondary market. The terms were much better than what Jeff had originally quoted. It was a no-brainer for the client to accept.

The other file was a unique situation. The documentation supplied ensured that the loan would not go south. The file contained a letter from the borrower's CPA stating that the client had ample resources to pay himself $800,000 annually. So far, so good. The challenge the underwriter had was that the customer only paid himself once a year. The CPA confirmed that the client had been paying himself in this manner for years. Jeff understood where the rub came in. He offered to sign a personal guarantee for six months using the funds from his Merrill Lynch account as collateral to alleviate the risk factor. This is when an unblemished reputation in your local market comes in handy. Although Jeff offered, the CEO said, "Don't worry about it." He wasn't concerned in the least. Knowing Jeff felt so strongly meant he could rest easy. He had total and complete faith in Jeff. That's how strong the owner of Guaranteed's trust was and still is. All eight loans closed within a forty-eight hour window. Not one of Jeff's customers missed their deadlines. The net result was that his borrowers never encountered a mortgage crisis, and they never felt their loan closing was at risk.

Without question, Guaranteed Rate passed Jeff's litmus test. Feeling confident that the CEO was a man of his word, Jeff negotiated the terms under which he and his team would come to work there. After his requirements were agreed to, Jeff gathered his team together to discuss joining the organization.

After they completed their site visit, his team reached a unanimous agreement to move forward within half an hour. As of this publication, The Lake Team continues to work out of the same location in Deerfield, a suburb of Chicago, providing the same excellent service they always have.

Groucho Marx said, "The secret of life is honesty and fair dealing. If you can fake that, you've got it made." Jeff Lake has never faked anything, and he never will.

THE OCCI METHOD: OBSERVE, CONTEMPLATE, CONCEIVE, AND IMPLEMENT

Told to and shared by Cindy

———— ❧ ————

Never look down on anyone unless you're helping them up.

—JESSE JACKSON

TIMELINE	EMPLOYER	ROLE
During the 2007–2008 Financial Crisis	American Home Mortgage	Branch Manager
Present Employer 2017	Broadview Mortgage	Sales Manager

WHEN I ORIGINALLY sat down to write this chapter, my focus was going to be on Julie's organizational skills and the results of the systems she implements at every step. We will still highlight her effectiveness in those areas; however, it would be a disservice to stop at this level. Julie Miller brings much more to the table than her methodologies. She brings her heart and soul to every client she works with. Julie has a very clear picture of her purpose and how that affects each person she has the ability to impact. She is a passionate woman who walks her talk every minute of every day.

The people Julie serves are important to her. Their welfare is her primary concern. She doesn't think of them as another loan. Rather, she sees a family that has their own unique story filled with dreams. It's an honor for her to play such an important role in the shaping of their future for many generations.

Some might conclude that Julie Miller's entrance into the mortgage industry began with a chain of events that could happen to anyone. However, I believe they were preordained to occur exactly the way they manifested. Would Julie have built her present model otherwise? Probably. It's who she is at the core of her being. It just might not have happened so early in her life.

THE NATURE OF THE BUSINESS

So what helped shape Julie's thought process? It was her own experience when she bought her first home in 1991. She was in her late twenties. Her parents had given her the down payment she needed as a gift to help her get started on the path to homeownership. She reached out to her junior high school friend who was in the mortgage business to help her with the financing. What could be better? She'd known him forever and trusted him. When he advised her that an adjustable rate mortgage (ARM) was the way to go, she accepted the loan terms without question. It never crossed Julie's mind to ask if there were other programs available.

A little more than two years after she bought her home, Julie ran into him at Diedrich Coffee in Orange County. While they were catching up, her friend encouraged her to think about a career as a loan officer. He thought she had the talent and the personality to be incredibly successful in the mortgage business. His persistence and winning personality were hard to resist, and in 1993, Julie joined him at California Mortgage Service.

During the time Julie studied, took the real estate salesperson test, and waited for the results, she received some on-the-job training. This is where she learned about the various types of loan programs available. It's also when Julie became aware that she could have had financing that had level payments and remained fixed over the entire life of the loan. Because of her lack of knowledge, she accepted a rate and payment that had the potential to increase on an annual basis. She was certain that if the fixed rate option had been presented to her, she would have taken it.

Not one to shy away from tough conversations, Julie asked her friend, now her boss, about the loan product he'd recommended. She wanted to know why he hadn't given her other options to consider. Rather than feeling contrite, he told Julie that if she was really unhappy she could refinance out of the present loan any time she wanted to. He really didn't understand where she was coming from. Today, some might not understand his attitude; however, at that time, it wasn't unheard of to rewrite a client's mortgage frequently.

Although Julie would have handled her transaction differently, she found her friend to be an excellent manager. He allowed her entrepreneurial spirit to thrive. From day one, Julie created a system for every aspect of her job. If something wasn't working smoothly, she added, removed, or refined until all worked as she envisioned. This diligence resulted in Julie's production growing rapidly. A year later, her manager accepted a new opportunity with North American Mortgage Company. He asked Julie to join him, which she did, without hesitation.

One day, while Julie was shopping at the Gap, she felt that the sales associate helping her would make an excellent assistant. Julie asked her if she would consider a change in profession. After receiving an affirmative answer, they met, and worked out the details. Her choice was a success. During our interview, I asked Julie why she'd felt comfortable taking a risk on someone with no mortgage experience. She said that large retail stores provide excellent training in customer service and the handling of objections. Not long after, Julie hired a second person to further boost the team's capacity.

In May 1998, a little more than a year after she hired her second assistant, Julie was introduced to Alison Bond, who became her third. The person she'd hired from the Gap had left at this point. Alison also had worked at a retail clothing store. She, too, had a great attitude, a high aptitude for learning, and *no* desire to become a commissioned salesperson. These traits are key. In fact, so much so that Julie continues to use the same criteria.

Alison's role as the team's transaction coordinator is to proactively communicate with all parties once they enter into contract or start their refinance. Proactive is the operative word here. Alison reaches out before someone feels the need to pick up the phone. If an inbound call involves a question related to status or what happens next, it means the ball was dropped. Alison takes her responsibility very seriously, which ensures closings happen *on time* and *stress-free*.

TRANSITION

Dime Bancorp, Inc., acquired North American Mortgage shortly after the group moved to the new company. The culture underwent a major shift. Rather than maintaining an intimate family vibe among the staff, the atmosphere became more corporate. Management required structure and conformity. The leadership was no longer willing to let branch managers remain autonomous in the running of their branches. This lack of freedom prompted her friend and mentor to retire around 1999. Julie, however, remained working as a loan officer for North American until she accepted a management position with Marina Mortgage in October 2000. Later American Home Mortgage (AHM) would acquire Marina, with Julie staying on as the branch manager.

By 2003, Julie's customer base had become substantial. To keep service levels up to her standards, they needed to add another person. Looking back, Julie wishes she'd made the decision to bring on another team member much earlier. As phenomenal as her growth had been up to that point, Julie now believes her ability to help others would have increased dramatically if she'd taken this leap sooner. Ivette Reynoso was hired in February of that same year. Her title today is CFO, Chief Follow-Up Officer. She stays in touch with *everybody* until they find a home.

The process starts with Ivette having a phone appointment with the borrower. She enters the information they share with her on to the intake form the team created. Ivette obtains a verbal authorization to order the credit report during this session. She also gives them a list of items needed to prepare them for their appointment with Julie. Ivette will be the main point of contact until the borrower has found a home to purchase. She is also a resource for those customers who need more time to get all their ducks in a row. Her other primary responsibility is to manage Julie's calendar, making sure she has ample time with the customer and there is enough leeway in between meetings. This keeps Julie on time, *always.*

One mini-system the Miller Team implemented early on (and still use today) is their introduction call with the real estate agents associated with the transaction. If either of the agents hasn't worked with them before, Julie will be the one to reach out and introduce herself. She takes the time to explain who's on her team and what their respective roles are. At the end of the call, the agent will have a clear understanding how Julie's process works, and all their questions will be answered. Those who have a previous relationship with Julie will receive a notification from Ivette indicating that the Miller Team has been hired to provide the financing.

These three women continue to run a very well-oiled machine. So well-oiled, in fact, that they felt only minor repercussions from the 2007–2008 meltdown, even though the unemployment rate shot up from 3.1 percent in December 2006 to its highest level of 10 percent in October 2009. That's because the Miller team has never offered high-risk, subprime, or predatory products. Borrowers are placed into loans that they can afford while meeting their financial objectives.

As the market got back on track, Julie felt it was time to hire an additional person to maintain customer satisfaction at stellar levels. Collectively, the team agreed that they needed someone in the area of guidelines and compliance. Research in this area was taking up an increasing amount of Julie's time. Each down payment assistance program (DPA) had its own set of unique caveats and nuances.

At the end of 2010, Julie hired Melissa Johnston to fill this void. She was a Regional Credit Manager (underwriter) for Marina Mortgage. She stayed with them after they fell under the American Home umbrella. When Melissa came to work with Julie, she had twenty-three years experience as an underwriter. What really drew Julie to Melissa was her friendly attitude and strong work ethic. Her extensive knowledge of Down Payment Assistance programs, and mainstream product guidelines makes her well suited for her current role on the Miller Team as the Loan Approval Specialist. She pre-approves every client based on Julie's recommendations, and reviews every file before it's submitted for approval. She's essentially the under-writer before the official underwriter. With the addition of Melissa, Julie rarely needs to be involved in the file after the initial consultation. She feels blessed to have surrounded herself with what she considers to be the very best talent available.

Julie's passion remains as strong today as when she first entered the lending profession more than two decades ago. From the day she vowed to look after those desiring homeownership, she began embracing these guiding principles:

- ◆ Recommendations are always in the best interest of the customer.

- ◆ Treat all parties involved fairly.

- ◆ Educate, educate, educate.

In Julie's estimation, it's a disservice not to inform individuals of the options available to them. No one should be kept in the dark just because it's easier. The chain of events that happened during her first purchase formed her desire to be an advocate for her clients. That's why from the very start of her career, she made the conscious decision to offer Down Payment Assistance (DPA) and the Mortgage Credit Certificate (MCC) programs. Although these require extra time, effort, and finesse, Julie doesn't mind at all. Helping others is in complete alignment with her values. It doesn't matter that the compensation is less or that going through various calculations to determine eligibility is more time-consuming.

Julie's belief in looking out for her customers reminds me of an excerpt I read in *High Trust Selling*," written by my friend Todd Duncan. The chapter titled "The Law of the Dress Rehearsal" does a phenomenal job of capturing the essence of her philosophy. In particular these two lines: "The key to selling is not selling; it's in providing, and the key to providing is in knowing in advance what to provide."

The net result of Julie and her team's efforts is an annuity-based business. They've created a legacy of happy financially secure homeowners, a group that has since evolved into a clientele with different needs from when they did their first loan with her. This translates into move-up buyers, vacation home purchases, and expanded real estate portfolios from the acquisition of investment properties.

TEACH, COUNSEL: SETTING CLIENTS UP FOR SUCCESS

Although Julie's business card reflects her official title as Sales Manager, her role is much more significant than that. She also performs and excels as a teacher and counselor. Julie spends a considerable amount of time educating her clientele, so they have the tools to make wise, informed decisions. Always. There are rare cases when the borrower chooses to go with a competitor. In those instances, it's not uncommon for them to come back to her later for their new financing needs.

Julie believes that all mortgage loan originators should take the time to counsel their clients on the cause and effect of their financial choices and actions. Based on the feedback she has received throughout the years, most don't do this. In her opinion, this conversation needs to happen whether it's a budding relationship or one that has existed for a long time. It doesn't matter if it's the borrower's first home or a subsequent one. Any increase in monthly spending that's significant will affect the borrower's current monthly budget.

It's her belief that most consumers dedicate more time developing their grocery list than they do preparing for financial independence and peace of mind. Sound familiar? It's the same thing Greg Frost found to be true. In the case of first-time homebuyers, in particular, she spends additional time helping families develop a budget for unplanned expenses. Roof repairs, plumbing and electrical expenses, appliance replacement, and, in some cases, even car repairs, can wreak havoc on the family budget. By taking the time to address these potential unexpected expenditures, borrowers put themselves in the driver's seat, instead of becoming victims of circumstances beyond their control. The time she spends counseling her clients helps set them up for success. Julie continues where Ivette left off by obtaining the borrowers thoughts to the questions listed below:

- How much money do they need to have in the bank to feel financially secure?

- Are both spouses (if applicable) on the same page when it comes to financial goals and reserves?

- Are there other expenses such as private schooling, day care, or saving for college education(s) that are a high priority now or will be in the near future?

Just like your doctor, Julie doesn't offer a diagnosis before she has gathered the preliminary information to do so. She uses the answers to the above questions as a guide to prescribe the right loan solution for the customer. In her opinion, she'd be shortchanging her clients if she relied solely on the documentation they provided, and the information obtained from the credit agencies. Without this feedback, she would be providing cookie-cutter solutions instead of personalized recommendations. Most people don't expect this level of care, nor do they know to ask for it. That's why every person who's fortunate enough to have received Julie's name as a resource is in a better position than when they started.

She has had her processes in place long before the Federal Reserve Board (FRB) proposed the Ability-to-Repay (ATR) rule on April 19, 2011. It's not that she's clairvoyant; rather, her heart has always been in the right place.

For those unfamiliar with the ATR rule, Section 1411, spells out the requirements lenders and creditors must adhere to when reviewing asset, employment, and income stability. In summary, the rule states when evaluating an applicant's creditworthiness the creditor must determine that it's reasonable to expect that the borrowers have the ability to repay all current debts, including the new financing, not just now, but in the future if nothing unforeseen occurs. The government felt the need to impose these regulations to ensure that the American public is not put in a position to fail. Julie could have been the author of this regulation many years in advance, perhaps even when we first met in 2002.

STREAMLINED SYSTEMS

We had our first meeting on October 3, 2002, to discuss how the firm I owned at the time, CD Consulting Group, could optimize the team's database efforts. Later, once we were under contract, I spent many days at the Miller Team's location. I witnessed how they treated one another and how their systems rolled out. What really stuck out to me was the calm and serene atmosphere in the office. There wasn't a whisper of tension, not an inkling of stress. Here was a team closing $60 million in volume annually, which equated to 300+ units, and everyone involved had a positive, remarkable experience.

By that point, I'd worked with hundreds of clients, and I had never run into that level of efficiency before. It seemed in Julie's world, the only purpose of an inbound phone call was either an inquiry to obtain financing or someone who had a referral in need of Julie's services. "Impressive" doesn't adequately describe what I witnessed.

There is no doubt about it; our first session was somewhat unconventional. Earlier in the morning prior to our meeting, I had taken Oscar the boxer, my six-month-old granddog (that's right, granddog) to our veterinarian located in Rim Forest, California, a very rural community. He said my son's puppy was in a lot of pain and needed to see a specialist right away. The office the vet recommended was near Julie's location. I called her to explain my situation and asked if we could reschedule our meeting for another day. "Nonsense," she said, "just bring Oscar with you after your appointment," and so I did. I can't remember ever bringing a pet with me to a client's office before or since. Julie's incredibly attuned to people's feelings. She knew how torn up I felt about Oscar and the need to reschedule our meeting on such short notice. Instead of postponing, she provided a solution that worked for both us.

After introducing him to dog-lover Julie, we dug into the purpose of our two-hour visit: to map out ways we could streamline her current processes. She was using a customized version of Goldmine™—a CRM powered by FrontRange Solutions™—to manage her communication with borrowers, agents, and third-party vendors involved on active transactions. Julie had invested heavily in this software with the expectation that it would increase the team's capacity.

The challenge lay in the amount of manual effort that was required to prevent interruptive, reactive calls. The good news was that we could automate many of their processes. However, to have that level of sophistication, my firm needed to refine some of the existing workflows they had in place and build a few more. Add-on products also needed to be purchased to enhance the program's out of the box features.

By May 2003, the above was in place. Together we built the content for additional auto-responders. The body of the e-mail templates were based on the recipient's response, or lack thereof, making the materials that were sent out more relevant and precise. What made Julie's system special is the amount of thought behind the correspondence. It didn't feel canned. The nature of the relationship the customer had with her also affected the wording. Below are examples of how Julie categorized prospect and borrower marketing campaigns:

- Prior to loan: leads and prospects.

- Active clients: current purchase and refinance transactions.

- Closed clients: referral opportunities and milestone recognition.

Professional associations were as follows:

- Brand new: listing or buyer agent listed on purchase contract.

- Existing relationship: worked with before.

- Strategic partner: reciprocal admiration and referral process.

To remove duplication of efforts, one of the products we incorporated had the ability to seamlessly integrate the data between the Loan Origination Software (LOS) and Goldmine. Most of the time, it was more efficient to export the information stored in the CRM and have it import into the LOS than it was to create a new loan application, since most of the client's information was stored there first. From that point on, data such as loan terms and dates indicating the status of the file were exported from the LOS and imported into the CRM. This synchronization happened in the background seamlessly.

The other major need Julie had was to enhance the reports she was currently pulling from her contact manager. We recommended Crystal Reports", a program that provides in-depth reporting capabilities, and is easily customizable. Here are a few examples of the reports (and one template) they still use with modifications:

+ **The Referral Source In** tracks the source of where all referrals originated, allowing Julie to determine which professional partners provide the highest quality of referrals. It also enables her to coach those who provide weaker ones, improving the rate of conversion.

+ **The Referral Source Out** monitors the stage of all referrals that the team provides to their strategic partners. Julie keeps a tight fist on the quality of service her clientele receives. She wants to make sure they're all getting the attention they deserve. Each referral she gives out is an extension of herself. Julie expects her professional partners to handle her borrowers with kid gloves.

+ **The Annual Review** keeps a record of closing date anniversaries, sorting them by month. The CRM sends a form to the client via e-mail asking if there have been any changes in their life since they last spoke with Julie. Ivette will simultaneously receive a task on her calendar. Even if the customer doesn't reply, Ivette still reaches out to update their information and schedule their annual review with Julie. This meeting is as important as the discovery session they had with Julie initially. The client may have had life events that warrant the restructuring of their loan. Or there could have been a recent change in regulations that merits a refinance. For example, the county loan limits increase, taking a high balance or jumbo loan amount to conforming limits. In this circumstance, the client is eligible for a reduced rate. Another instance that makes a rewrite viable is when property values go up enough to remove private mortgage insurance. Julie feels every borrower deserves and is entitled to this level of service. The report provides the information at a glance making it a significantly less arduous process for Julie to deliver on her commitment.

- **The Birthday Review** really helps Ivette in her fulfillment duties. Similar to the previous report, client birthdays are sorted in chronological order. This allows her to prepare birthday cards in advance ensuring they're mailed in a timely fashion.

- **The Weekly Status** is an e-mail generated from a template. Its purpose is to update all parties with the progress of the loan since the previous week's communication. Recipients are told when services or documents have been ordered, are expected back, or have been received from third-party vendors: escrow, title, and the appraiser.

    Critical milestone dates are also provided—including the date the loan is submitted to underwriting, receives approval, and has reached cleared to close (CTC) status. It also lists when final loan documents are ordered, signed, and received from the closing agent. Each party is sent their own individual e-mail every Friday, automatically when the blast is launched.

Julie continued to use the customizations we built for her in 2003 until the early part of 2013. Eventually, though, Goldmine wasn't equipped to handle the complexity that Julie required. She has since switched systems. After looking at numerous programs, she invested in a lender version of Salesforce™ designed by Mike Gulitz, the founder and CEO of Jungo™. The name of the product originally was Mortgage Planner CRM. Julie learned of the program at Sales Mastery,™ where she was one of the featured speakers. What caught her interest initially was the dashboard, which contained everything she needed at a glance. It was also easily configurable, which means the creation of automated daily workflows for the team wasn't going to be nearly as arduous or expensive as her previous system. The other feature Jungo had that was high on her list was the ability to access her database from the cloud. Prior to this, the team had to be in the office to view the database. Julie's thrilled with their customer support, which she states is off the charts.

From the day Julie entered the mortgage profession, she's remained devoted to the creation and maintenance of her systems. I admire this about her. She leaves nothing to chance, and nothing happens by accident. Her standard operating procedure has always been to:

+ Observe

+ Contemplate

+ Conceive

+ Implement

I call it her OCCI method. When asked why it's *so* difficult for some people to get systems off the ground and keep them running smoothly, Julie indicated that salespeople make them too grandiose, too complex, and they contain far too many steps. This often means hiring additional staff, which can become cost-prohibitive. In her estimation, simplicity is the key to implementation.

Julie is not a procrastinator. She takes action. Rather than tabling what needs fixing, the Miller Team follows the above steps, laying the groundwork for corrective action immediately. If at any point there's an indication their system isn't operating at optimal performance, the team sets time aside to brainstorm. What they don't do is wait for a situation to become magnified, causing a plethora of unhappy customers. An example of some of the questions they ask themselves are:

+ What could we have done differently to prevent stuff from slipping through the cracks?

+ Do we need to refine, remove, or add another step?

- Should we have communicated sooner?

- Did we use the best method of communication?

After American Home closed their doors in 2007, Julie joined Prospect Mortgage. She worked there until she accepted an opportunity with Broadview Mortgage Corporation in 2013. Her team has followed her through all these transitions, which she greatly appreciates. Julie places team stability high on her priority list. Without them, it would be very difficult, if not impossible, for her to have a balanced life along with her success. She is able time to spend with her three incredible and very active boys. Julie loves watching their water polo matches and cherishes the time she spends with them. Her desire for helping people with affordable home-ownership has continued to shine rather than dim throughout the years. Do you have the same passion driving you? If so, let it shine!

LARRY BETTAG

TEEC: TRUST, EDUCATION, EFFICIENCY, AND CONSISTENCY

Told to and shared by Cindy and Kathleen

———————✖———————

An investment in knowledge pays the best interest.

—BENJAMIN FRANKLIN

TIMELINE	EMPLOYER	ROLE
During the 2007–2008 Financial Crisis	Cherry Creek Mortgage	Branch Manager
Present Employer 2017	Cherry Creek Mortgage	Regional Vice President

HOW DOES A PERSON with a master's degree in clinical psychology segue into becoming a mortgage lender with a Doctor of Jurisprudence, specializing in real estate law? It helps to understand what mattered most to Larry Bettag as a young adult. He began his diverse education by obtaining his Bachelor of Arts degree from Benedictine University in 1985 with an emphasis in literature and communication.

To earn extra pin money during his undergrad years, Larry took a job as a counselor at Camp St. Malo in Allenspark, Colorado. This is where he spent his days every summer. The camp's mission is to help children from ages eight to sixteen who have had to endure difficult upbringings. Some come from abusive households, while others have had different challenges beyond their control that they need to overcome. The camp believes that spending time outdoors fosters the healing process.

Summer became a time of inspiration for Larry as he developed a strong sense of admiration for these young people. Working at the camp was more than just a way to spend the summer; he truly loved every one of those kids. When a camper prepared to leave, Larry vowed to stay in touch with them when he returned to the fall semester. He provided his address, indicating he would write back to anyone who took the time to correspond with him. During those four years, Larry received as many as six letters a day from the campers. Today, he still maintains relationships with fourteen individuals he met during that period of his life. The bonds forged during those summer months enabled Larry to witness firsthand the power of healing, inspiration, and personal growth, which he considers one of the greatest influences in his life. This experience is what guided him to obtain his master's degree in clinical psychology from Roosevelt University.

After his graduation, Larry obtained a job in his field with a local counseling firm that ran a family and marriage practice. Originally, he intended to work with children. Instead, the ratio of clients Larry worked with was one child to every twenty-nine couples who had marital problems. He found that two-thirds of them had no real desire to work toward saving their marriages and were only interested in playing the blame game. Instead of feeling the gratification he expected to from his days at St. Malo, Larry dreaded going to work. Each day felt like a repeat of the same old, same old.

Based on his dissatisfaction with his experience in the counseling profession, Larry concluded his life needed an in-flight correction. After careful deliberation, he decided to earn his law degree and immediately enrolled at Northern Illinois University, attending full-time. Before long, Larry arrived at the same consensus his fellow undergraduates had when they had entered into the law program. The purpose of the first year is to scare the student to death. Will they do what it takes to be successful? Just as the St. Malo campers had to dig from within when climbing the tough terrain of the Rocky Mountains, so did the first-year law students as they navigated their professors' questions and exams.

They found themselves buried with even more work the second year. Instead of slowing down the pace, the course load increased. In addition to the grueling amount of study, individuals were encouraged to participate in moot court, work at legal aid clinics, and write for law reviews and journals. It's understood that those who keep their noses to the grindstone, stay disciplined, and take on these added responsibilities will enjoy the fruits of their hard work—landing jobs at more prestigious law firms. The strategy makes sense. After all, law isn't a profession where you wing it. Dedication, conscientiousness, and diligence are crucial.

The third and final year of law school, from the students' perspective, is to bore them to death. This was certainly true for Larry, who felt there had been so much heavy lifting in the first two years that his last year felt repetitive and no longer fresh. It was during this time that his friend suggested he consider becoming a loan officer. She felt the combination of his communication skills, counseling background, and education in real estate law were the perfect ingredients for a very successful career in mortgage banking.

OFF WE GO AS A LO

At first, Larry completely rejected his friend's suggestion. The idea was not at all palatable to him. His paternal grandfather, father, and three brothers were all MDs. On his maternal side, his grandfather and uncles were either lawyers or judges. Clearly, there was no family history when it came to sales. Larry had always bought into the stereotype of the used-car salesman. He told his wife, Michelle, that he just could not get past that image.

Then one day, he had an epiphany. Larry realized that *everyone's* in sales, including his social circle—priests, teachers, fellow students, even his family and friends were in sales. His big "aha" was three-fold. First, the individuals who were successful in sales believed strongly in what they promoted. Second, they approached everything from a place of wanting to be of service. Larry describes people with this attitude as having a "servant's heart." Whereas if the salesperson he dealt with had a "What's in it for me?" approach, the deal didn't happen. Third, and most important, they were not simply trying to close a sale, but were wanting to bring value to the relationship. Repeatedly he saw that whenever he bought into anyone or anything, these three factors were always present. With his newfound insight, Larry accepted a position in 1994 as a loan officer at Norwest, where he worked while finishing up his final semester of law school.

STARTING OVER

The following September, Larry obtained a position as a litigator with Shearer & Agrella, the oldest law firm in Kane County, Illinois. He concentrated in real estate contracts and litigation. Even though he was enjoying his position at Norwest, he'd just invested a considerable amount of time and money into becoming an attorney and wasn't about to throw it all away.

Instead of choosing one, Larry decided to work at both places. As of this publication and since passing the bar exam, he limits his caseload to two or three active clients. This enables him to balance his time at the firm while meeting the requirements to keep his license to practice law active.

From the time he started at Norwest, Larry devoted forty to sixty hours per week. Within four years, he'd been promoted to sales manager and headed the largest producing team, for the company's number one branch nationwide. Larry's leadership skill and gracious manner cultivated an environment that individuals wanted to be a part of.

The merger of Norwest and Wells Fargo was announced in June 1998 and completed in November of that year. The branch retained the Norwest name for about a year before switching over to Wells Fargo. The two entities could not have had more contrasting cultures. Norwest had a reputation as a friendly, high-touch organization with terrific customer service. They were also known for their superior sales culture. While Wells, staring bankruptcy in the face, had the opposite reputation. What they did bring to the table was their cutting-edge technology and online presence. Norwest's rationale for the merger was to take advantage of both these attributes while increasing their cross-sell opportunities, among other reasons.

By the time 2000 rolled around, Larry was feeling the negative effects of the acquisition. His branch had dwindled from fifty-five employees to five, including himself. Despite his many promotions, Larry felt he could not be effective when there was no team to lead. The mass exodus that had occurred in less than a year indicated to him that the Wells Fargo platform was no longer desirable. He knew a change in employers was inevitable and started to focus on finding a new home.

Larry interviewed with seventeen companies before joining Cherry Creek Mortgage. Although he traveled far down the interview path with a few firms, most did not pique his interest. Often, it came down to just a gut feeling that a particular company was not the right fit, even with a great leader at the helm. It was clear that his interviewers had researched his ability to close loans, and lead people or they would not have spent time courting him. But Larry felt they did not see the kind of man he was, nor did they care. Many of the firms he had conversations with were more concerned with emphasizing their underwriting times, ease of closing, competitive rates, and attractive commission schedules.

They did not ask him any questions. Instead, they simply talked *at* him and told him why they would be the best organization for him to join. From his perspective, it appeared all they were after was a revenue-generating machine. Larry wanted to be with a company that took interest in him as an individual and did not just see him as a loan-producing widget. He already knew how it felt to be invisible after the Wells Fargo merger, and he knew without question he didn't want to spend the majority of his waking hours in that type of environment.

The Executive Vice President of Cherry Creek Mortgage Company, Stacey Harding, conducted his meeting with Larry in a completely different style. Instead of bragging about what his establishment had to offer, Stacey was genuinely interested in getting to know him. He wanted to know about the situations where Larry felt his previous employers had let him and his team down, how he chose to handle those frustrations, and what his goals were for himself and his family. Equally as important to Stacey, if not more so, was finding out what Larry's passions were. He wanted to identify with what excited him, what got Larry up in the morning, what made him tick. As their conversations continued over several sessions, it became evident to Stacey that Larry would bring tremendous value to his company. Larry came to feel that Stacey was a leader he could thrive under and learn a great deal from. He felt there was mutual trust and that Stacey would bring out the best in him.

During his due diligence process, Larry was encouraged by what he learned about his future employer. Having started as a three-person mortgage office in 1987, the firm had come from humble beginnings. This quote from the executive summary—on a recent version of the company website— exemplifies the company's tenets: "[Cherry Creek] consists of a collection of individuals who understand the greatness that transpires when everyone does their best. Honor and integrity are essential. They demand everyone give their personal and professional best. It's in this spirit that our team members pledge their best in an effort to create something great in the lives of others."

Both Stacey and Larry had the same goal in mind: culture fit. Stacey understood how important it was for members of the Cherry Creek family to have parallel values and principles. There had to be an ethics match. Without these similar philosophies and ideologies, experience had shown employees would move on. Larry felt the company culture was in alignment with what he was seeking. He'd found an organization that felt like home to him. Eighteen years later, Larry's still grateful to be a part of such an altruistic firm.

In addition to working as a Regional Vice President for Cherry Creek *and* practicing law, Larry is also a builder—a constructer of relationships, contacts, and reputation. He discovered that what really mattered most in mortgage sales is *relationships* and *trust*; so he emphasizes education and investing in the success of others. He feels strongly this is the number one way he is able to help people move from a position of vulnerability to one of empowerment. This isn't limited to borrowers and professional partners; education is how Larry helps anyone he has the ability to touch.

MAKING THE ROUNDS

Larry learned the value of "making rounds" from observing both his anesthesiologist dad, and later, his oncologist brother, Steven. This is why he adopted a doctor's style of visitation. He kept his routine consistent, visiting (or "rounding") the real estate offices every Thursday and Friday. Larry continued this practice with regularity until he became a regional manager with seventeen branches under his belt.

He understands that the old adage "out of sight, out of mind" appropriately describes the ramifications one risks when taking the customer for granted. He believes it's *imperative* that originators stay in front of their agents, because, if they don't, there are many contenders out there vying for the opportunity to become a salesperson's replacement.

With that said, not all agents are a good fit with every loan officer, team, or company. Rather than casting a wide net and trying to garner work from everyone, Larry highly recommends going through an interview process with potential professional partners to find an essence match, meaning someone with similar values. In his case, Larry searches for, and is proud to work with, agents who truly care about the clients they represent.

It's important to him that both he and his agents have mutual respect for one another. Without this, a relationship centered on trust cannot be founded, and is not sustainable. He has taught his team to anticipate loose ends, and then tie them up neatly to ensure the customer experience runs smoothly each time. Without this practice firmly ingrained into the process, the steady flow of business is in jeopardy. Larry and his group also embrace the notion that they are a direct reflection of the person who referred them. If the referral source shines, then the team has been effective in their role as ambassadors.

Larry has adhered to this rock-solid philosophy throughout his career. As a result, his business has continued to remain strong from the get-go. Rounding the bend of 2006, Larry and Michelle entered into a contract to construct an expensive home. For the first time in a long while, the Bettag's would be committed to a very sizeable mortgage. Previously, they had been debt-free, which helped them accumulate a healthy nest egg. Although the idea of incurring this obligation was scary, the market had been solid for so long that the couple decided to take the leap and build their dream home.

Larry's income had always been very stable until the end of 2007, when, for the first time ever, he encountered a month where his earnings dropped below the cost of maintaining his life style. He was used to a steady and consistent income flow. But suddenly, as the mortgage meltdown heated up, Larry encountered three months of declining income in a row. His new home was almost completed, with the permanent financing going into effect in thirty days. Larry was beyond nervous contemplating this huge financial commitment. Backing out of the transaction was not an option because he had already incurred the major part of the debt.

Larry believes he's fortunate to have a Type A, ADD personality. He goes through life at 100 mph. He could have let a sense of self-imposed paralysis freeze him, but he did not. Instead, he committed to what he calls "mandos." These are mandatory tasks that Larry considers non-negotiable. What's great about his mandos is that they don't require an enormous amount of time to complete. They do, however, require laser focus. Immediately Larry stepped up his efforts by increasing the frequency in which he reached out to his agent community, closed clients *and* any other individuals that had the influence to refer a steady stream of borrowers to him and his team.

Larry points out that while he is a bulldog concerning big-picture initiatives, because of his short-term focus, he knew he wouldn't spend two to three hours straight to accomplish the directives he set for himself. What he could commit to, however, was a series of mini tasks that he considered to be high pay-off activities over the course of a week. This is a critical point. Had Larry not recognized and accepted that his attention span was limited, he would have set himself up for failure. Instead, he built a business model that worked for him.

However, Larry knew these two steps alone would not be sufficient to achieve the high-speed liftoff he was looking for or the longevity he needed to weather the crisis and beyond. That is precisely the reason why he dug in his heels and became invested in his recruitment efforts. Larry strongly believes that fear is what incapacitates individuals, and it's the absolute worse emotional choice a person can make. Fear paralyzes, and it always results in regret. That is why he did not sit and stew about his situation; rather he found a way to change his current dynamic.

When asked if it had been difficult to recruit in the existing mortgage market conditions, Larry said that quite the opposite was true. In fact, it was surprisingly easier than he ever expected. Action fights fear. During this time, there was a lot of uncertainty. Loan officers were unhappy as a rule with their present situation. If they thought Larry or Cherry Creek could alleviate some of their pain, they were open to discussing options. These efforts, coupled with his perseverance, and the number of lenders closing their doors kept him out of what could have been a fiscally disastrous situation.

SOCIAL MEDIA=RELATIONSHIPS[10]

With his recruiting efforts moving full steam ahead, Larry determined that his next course of action was to support his growing team by beefing up production. Over time, he had observed that a shift was happening with consumers in general. More and more, they were accessing the Internet to garner information. Before making decisions, they were tapping into social media to get feedback from their friends. Gathering information wasn't restricted to an isolated set of topics but had spread to all areas of life, including real estate purchases and financing decisions.

Larry knew he had to embrace this change in the origination process if he wanted progressive growth. As with everything else, he committed to the process regardless of the initial results. He started out with posting blogs on ActiveRain about halfway through 2012. This gave him the ability to grow his online presence. At the onset, Larry created at least ten posts a week. His material focused on five main categories:

- ◆ Inspiration.

- ◆ Self-deprecating humor—the majority of his content.

- Personal pieces.

- Education—content covering both professional and life lessons.

- Sharing business successes—usually limited to one per week.

Posts that generated a lot of activity caused the Google search engine to move him up to the top of the list when people were looking for the type of information he provided. This heightened Larry's exposure to the public dramatically. Some of his most successful blog posts on ActiveRain included:

- Do Not Blow Up Your Closing before You Even Buy!

- Credit Inquiries DO MATTER!

- Sometimes . . . No Matter What . . . Home Buying Can Be Stressful.

The statistics from Larry's endeavors are impressive. The year prior to our interview Larry received 137 direct closings from his blog posts on ActiveRain. From those 137, he received an additional twenty-five recommendations. Of those leads, 30 percent converted within a ninety-day period, and 80 percent of all of them transitioned from lead status to closed business. On average, Larry has referred more than twenty real estate contracts to his agents annually for the last six years.

Larry warns that expecting a lot of immediate business from this activity isn't realistic. For the first six to nine months, he didn't receive a single referral from his online efforts. He just felt certain he was headed in the right direction. "Consistency is key; otherwise, you will lose momentum." Commit to the process and the results will come is the policy he embraces.

Because blogging during the day would take away from his work time, Larry spent forty-five to sixty minutes writing his posts at night, after his wife and kids went to bed. This enabled him to provide his followers with a daily dose of education or inspiration that was fresh and insightful on a consistent basis each morning. In fact, it was through one of these posts that Larry and I reconnected. I felt honored when he agreed to share his story with me.

Several years into his enormous success with ActiveRain, Larry encountered Internet problems at home. The situation prevented him from creating his evening posts. During the three months his Internet was down, he migrated to Facebook (though he still blogs, just not as frequently). He accessed this platform while he was at the office. Facebook has broadened his scope as he began to actively reach out to three different spheres:

♦ Personal friends

♦ Professional friends

♦ Those who want to become friends

Larry found that reconnecting with people from his past felt good. It also brings the added benefit of friends from as far back as high school reaching out to him for their financing needs. Employees from his company who are located in other parts of the country feel they know Larry on a personal level because of his efforts on social media. Even though they haven't physically met—and in some cases, believe it or not, haven't *even* spoken on the phone. This is why they recommend Larry when one of their clients or employees is relocating within his geographic region.

Larry believes Facebook creates transparency through public messaging, while also producing a level of reciprocal engagement. In addition to taking the time to post a message, Larry likes and shares other's posts, which demonstrates to his Facebook social circle that he's interested in what matters to them. In turn, they do the same for him.

It's important to point out that there are several universal laws Larry is accessing. These are what drive how a consumer makes purchasing decisions. The first law is that either people like you or they don't. Social media helps individuals make that determination before a relationship is established. Second, customers trust people they like. Third, most make a decision based on emotion. Future buyers are looking to eliminate the pain points in their lives, and the feedback from others helps them do that. Social media provides an individual an effective tool to build a personal brand while reaching a diverse and wide range of potential business at little or no cost.

This is why Larry saw the value of building an online strategy. He warns it's tempting to get too wrapped up in feeds and what's trending.

Larry spends approximately ten minutes a day on Facebook, and you will, too, once you formulate a rhythm. As evidenced by the amount of time Larry spends on this activity, it's *not* his core business model, but rather, only a small part of it. It's a way to create social proof and connect others who may not connect otherwise. That's a lot of traction for very little expense, if the audience is targeted strategically. Currently, Larry does not pay for advertising. Below is the revenue he's generated from his time commitment:

- 2017: $120,000

- 2106: $60,000

- 2015: $60,000

- 2014: $40,000

- 2013: $18,000

- 2012: 9,000

BRANCHING OUT

At the time of this writing, Larry oversees seven states, consisting of seventeen branches. Last year, his region produced $350 million in closed volume. Because of the duties his current role as Regional Vice President entails, he's needed to shift a large portion of how he spends his workweek. Although Larry has stepped away from originating he still creates leads for the loan originators that fall within his branch and region. But that's not all that he does to facilitate the growth of his team members.

Larry presently dedicates every Tuesday to mentoring those who wish to advance to a higher level. Similar to law school, this mentorship isn't for those that want to coast. Recipients of his time are 100 percent committed to working and staying focused on dollar-productive activities. Participants are expected to call twenty-five or more agents every Monday morning with the goal of solidifying an appointment. Just as in 2007, "rounding" is still a core tenet for creating and maintaining relationships. Once a month, mentees participate in a program dubbed Thirsty Thursday, a happy hour held at a local establishment. The purpose of this event is for the originators to have unfettered access to the real estate community. This enables them to develop bonds on a personal level.

So what else could a previously nationally ranked top twenty loan officer within his company, who later progressed to being a Regional Vice President, and real estate attorney decide to do to widen his horizons? He could write a book! And that's what he did. *No Rewind: Only One Shot* was published in 2014. The book is a collection of true stories from people who have made the decision to go from good to great. Larry wants readers to let go of excuses and start utilizing the gifts and talents they've been given. To do otherwise, he feels, is a waste.

In addition to writing his book, Larry became president of the Illinois Association of Mortgage Professionals, which later changed its name to Greater Midwest Lenders Association. During his tenure, he facilitated a change in the organization. Rather than just representing the state of Illinois, the association was revamped to embody the additional states of Indiana, Iowa, Kansas, Michigan, Minnesota, Missouri, Nebraska, North Dakota, South Dakota, Ohio, and Wisconsin.

Today, Larry's team consists of a couple of loan officers who have taken over his production. This allows him to stay focused on his mandos—those things that matter most to him. At work it's serving his branch managers, the loan officers within his region, and recruiting. The delegation of sales has allowed him more time with Michelle and their five children. Outside of work, Larry enjoys hiking the Rocky Mountain range, and as a former professional disc golfer he still plays rounds recreationally. To this day, Larry remains true to what he calls his Vince Lombardi mentality—God first, family second, Green Bay Packers, err . . . Cherry Creek Mortgage third.

MICHAEL DEERY

TURN COLD CALLS INTO HOT LEADS

Told to and shared by Cindy

———◆◆◆———

You miss 100% of the shots you do not take.

—WAYNE GRETZKY

TIMELINE	EMPLOYER	ROLE
During the 2007–2008 Financial Crisis	Citywide Financial Corp.	Non-Producing Owner
Present Employer 2017	Citywide Financial Corp.	Producing Owner

MICHAEL DEERY was born and raised on the northern coast of Ireland, in beautiful Donegal, surrounded by the friendliest and most helpful people in the world. He attributes his positive outlook on life to the environment he grew up in, including a family gifted with lots of jolly good fun and business acumen. The latter of which helped him develop his entrepreneurial spirit.

From a very early age, Michael developed a passion for competitive soccer. When he was just sixteen years old, he moved to England to play professionally for three years with the Liverpool team. The University of San Diego noticed his athleticism and offered him a soccer scholarship in 1994. Michael packed his bags, left England, and moved to the United States. He graduated in 1999 with a bachelor's degree in business and psychology.

His first job right out of college was with Norwest Financial. The branch would change their name within a few months of his hire date to reflect the Wells Fargo merger. During the year he worked there, his primary responsibility was to cold call people from the company database who were currently delinquent on their payments. Michael talked to them about ways they could get back on track. He continued to keep tabs on their accounts. Once customers were current, management expected Michael to steer them toward additional products that offered a higher yield for the bank. Credit cards, short-term installment loans for furniture, and car financing fit into this category. Talk about having to make a *tough* phone call. For borrowers who were paid as agreed, Michael started out by saying he was conducting a customer satisfaction survey. If they were happy he launched into marketing the products management expected him to sell. For those who weren't, Michael worked on resolving their issues. Once he was successful he followed the same procedure.

Michael became indoctrinated to the world of real estate financing as he overheard the originators sitting near him speaking on the phone to their clients. Sometimes their discussions involved going over the merits of their file with the underwriter. The more Michael heard, the more intrigued he became by the process. His interest was piqued to the point that he began asking questions, cataloguing what he learned into his mental filing system. One of the first things he wanted to know was how the earnings potential differed from company to company for a mortgage loan officer. He found out that a commissioned salesperson could make a substantially higher income than his $2,200 a month salary.

With this newfound knowledge, Michael decided he wanted a career in real estate financing. His first step was to perform some reconnaissance. He began by combing the yellow pages for companies that specialized in mortgages. Then he called every establishment that looked promising to find out about their offerings. Michael devoted several months to the investigative process during his time off.

When he first started making his inquiries, Michael had no desire for, or expectation of, changing jobs until he reached his one-year anniversary. He felt that if he left to take another job before then, future employers would be concerned with his stability.

Initially his questions were very basic. Were originators expected to have their own book of business, or was the company willing to groom individuals without experience? Did the organization attracted high producers, and what was it that appealed to them? He also wanted to know if the sales agents remained loyal, and why. Or if the opposite were true and there was a lot of turnover, why was that? Getting and tracking the answers to these elementary questions would help him narrow down which companies to focus on when he was ready.

As the twelve-month mark grew closer Michael began to get more granular with his inquiries. How did the company he was calling define a top producing loan officer? How many units were they closing? What type of customer did they attract? What was the average loan size? How big of a territory would he be given? What kind of support should he expect? After the initial dialogue, if both parties had an interest in each other, they would set up an interview.

The job search process may seem manual and tedious to some born to the digital age; however, the Internet and social media had not yet gained the traction they have today. Michael's efforts led him to a meeting with Household Finance Services. During his first interview, he learned that loan officers were earning $7,000 or more a month there! He was definitely interested, but to land the job, he had make it through three levels of interviews. His last meeting before getting hired was with the district manager, who happened to be a huge soccer fan. By the end of their meeting, the DM offered him the position of junior loan officer in the company's retail sector.

The timing worked out perfectly. Michael had just reached the one-year milestone he'd set for himself. He liked that the parent company, had acquired a large database of customers through their acquisition of Beneficial

Corporation a couple of years before in 1998. This brought an insurgence of credit card holders to Household's already healthy database.

DIVING IN

The company provided their loan officers access to the customer base. With his prior experience of reaching out to this type of consumer, Michael felt the transition to the new company wouldn't be a difficult one. These all started out as cold calls; however, Michael warmed them up by starting his interaction as a customer service inquiry, just as he had when he was with Wells Fargo.

Once he got a handle on their level of satisfaction, he determined what avenue the conversation would take. Michael encouraged people who were satisfied with their experience to discuss their current and future financial plans by asking open-ended questions. He would then segue into the next level of his dialogue.

If the individual already owned their home, he brought up the possibility of refinancing to either reduce their payments, pull out cash, or both. For others who were renting, he introduced the idea of homeownership. Either way, he positioned himself and his company as a resource. Before ending the call, Michael made sure to set a follow-up appointment with anyone interested in going on to the next step, eliminating the time-wasting cycle of voicemail tag. For those who were not ready to proceed, he requested permission to check back with them.

When granted, Michael would place a reminder in his calendar for making the next contact. He also made sure to send an e-mail directly following their conversation with a brief summary of what they'd talked about. Included in the body of the message was a request for the customer to confirm that they wanted Michael to remain in touch with them. The reason he did this additional step was to comply with the Gramm Leach Bliley Act (GLB), also known as the Financial Services Modernization Act of 1999. Besides being an extremely good practice, Michael put forth this extra effort so he could continue his solicitation. Otherwise, without written approval, he would have had to stop contacting the consumer after ninety days.

During our interview, when I asked Michael why more loan officers don't cold call, he said he believes it's because originators cannot get past their fear of rejection. As a result, they really handicap themselves. He feels most salespeople overthink the outcome causing them to procrastinate, or worse, never move forward at all. In his opinion, their actions seem to indicate they would rather construct reasons why they cannot make calls instead of just doing the deed.

Michael admits that in his youthful ignorance it never occurred to him to worry about that. He also acknowledges that his accent tended to help him break the ice. Nevertheless, even without his Irish brogue, he would have jumped in feet first. He had to get started somehow, and the phone provided him a way to do that. In his opinion, a "No" is not the end of the world. In fact, it's a good thing, because from his viewpoint every one of those negative responses brought him that much closer to his end goal of a "Yes." As far as he is concerned sales is always a numbers game. And the reality is, the more calls Michael made, the better he got at his delivery, improving his odds of getting a positive response.

After working as a junior loan officer for roughly a year and a half, Michael decided he wanted to become a master at his craft and switched gears. The catalyst that prompted him to apply for an account executive position happened when HSBC acquired Household Finance. The company had openings in their wholesale division, Decision One. The ability to add non-conforming mortgage programs, in addition to the standard "A" product he currently had, provided additional opportunities for him.

Michael worked in this role for nearly two years to broaden his experience. In addition to calling on brokers for their business he was expected to underwrite the loans he brought in. Michael gained a better understanding of what constituted an acceptable credit risk and which situations required additional steps for the borrower to follow in order to become creditworthy. With this experience under his belt, Michael felt strongly he was now in position to take the next step in his career.

STRIKING OUT

Tapping into his entrepreneurial spirit, Michael decided to start his own firm, Citywide Financial, which opened its doors March 17, 2004, on St. Patrick's Day, in honor of his Irish heritage. Twenty-one loan officers, whom he had established a relationship with from his time at Decision One, approached him over a period of time to join his new company. Michael concentrated his efforts on coaching and training his staff while he continued to promote growth through his recruitment efforts. Business grew, and within six months, there were more than thirty-five loan officers working at Citywide. Occasionally, one of his clients from his time working as a retail loan officer reached out to him for assistance with their financing needs. If he had the time, Michael would write the loan, but since it wasn't his primary focus, he often referred these deals to one of his originators.

Approximately two years after Michael opened his doors, the volume of business had escalated. He was at to the point where he needed to hire additional resources to process the loans in the pipeline. Michael needed a well-versed processor who not only knew underwriting guidelines, but also had the customer service skills he required to meet his high standards. He had remained in contact with many of his colleagues from his previous employer, including one of their branch managers, Hallie Palacios, whom he held in high esteem. He was confident that she would be the perfect addition to Citywide. His recruiting efforts paid off; she joined the team in 2006 as their processing manager.

STARTING OVER

A few months after the company's four-year anniversary, the mortgage meltdown reared its ugly head. There had been evidence that the market was in trouble by the middle of 2007, but it wasn't until 2008 that the team members of Citywide Financial personally felt the brunt of the financial crisis. For months, cash flow had been declining at a rapid rate. By the time Michael paid existing commissions, salaries, insurance, and all the other expenses associated with running his mortgage company, he had no extra money to set aside for reserves; and he needed those reserves, especially during this difficult time.

Michael hadn't paid himself for several months. His ethics wouldn't allow him to do so until he'd paid his staff and met his credit obligations. Michael's stress level was off the charts; his life was out of control. He decided to restructure his business, which was probably the hardest call he's ever had to make. Michael said it was the worst experience of his life was when he had to let twelve people go in one day and another thirteen the following week. He felt he had no choice if he wanted to save the company.

One of the first major shifts Michael made was to refocus all his efforts on growing his own pipeline. That meant concentrating all his energy on what he could control, that is, himself. For years, he'd attempted to mentor the sales team. Some had listened, but most were very lax with their execution. With the exception of a few select loan officers who demonstrated they were truly self-reliant, the only staff member Michael held onto was Hallie. Having her, as his processor was instrumental in helping him to rebuild his business.

On the surface, the odds of renewed success seemed unattainable. Yet crazy as it seems, the financial crisis provided the catalyst that literally transformed how Michael would attract and conduct business, then and now.

Often, when the chips are down, we, as humans, have a habit of looking for the magic pill that will get us out of the mess we are facing, rather than taking the time to focus on what will change the reality of our current situation. Michael knew he had the desire, determination, and perseverance to succeed. Most of all, he could count on himself to stay motivated and on track to perform the activities that would earn him a robust practice once again.

Michael reflected on the future he wanted until it was crystal clear in his mind. With his vision intact, he built a game plan that in his estimation separated him from the competition. It started with changing the perception his borrowers and professional partners currently had of him. He wanted to elevate his persona to being *the* resource for real estate financing, rather than just another loan officer on the streets asking for business.

Previously, before the crisis, Michael thought having a swank storefront was the way to go. However, in his new reality, he understood this wasn't necessary. In fact, he realized he was limiting himself when he restricted his visibility solely to foot traffic. No, Michael was looking to engage a much larger audience. To achieve the kind of presence he was looking for, he needed to establish himself on the Internet so people who needed his solutions could locate him right away.

From his research, Michael learned that once visitors came to his site, he had only a few seconds to grab and capture their interest. He needed an abundance of content that was broad enough in scope to satisfy a diverse audience. To provide extra value, his material needed to be cutting-edge *and* not readily available from other sources. Michael's goal was to be the trendsetter, not a trend follower. In his estimation, this is what would keep people coming back. Michael's brilliant strategy boiled down to the simple, yet effective formula below:

Attract Traffic → Deliver Value without Strings → Begin Courtship

His posted material is what would originally draw the viewer in. They'd be able to garner information without having to disclose anything about themselves. Once a person chose to download material their level of engagement was increasing, which meant so was their trust. That's when the courtship really began. As long as his materials remained relevant to those who accessed his site, they'd be more likely to become subscribers. Once an individual elected to opt-in to receive his information, their status elevated beyond anonymous. The dating cycle was entering into the early stages of a professional relationship getting ready to form. If the recipient was looking forward to getting his information, then it stood to reason they'd start to think of Michael as their resource in all things mortgage-related, which aligned with his vision. As time evolved and he had a better understanding of the customer's needs. His materials would become more individualized, making them more and more personal, which strengthened the rapport. The nurturing phase remains in effect from the initial subscription, continuing through the engagement of services, and the remainder of the relationship. It's an essential component that keeps the bond in tact between him and the customer. Whether Michael realized it or not, he was following the tenets of Seth Godin's book, *Permission Marketing*.

Early on, Michael realized that building the volume of pertinent information would be a momentous job. It would require discipline and consistency, qualities inherent to his genetic make-up. The same traits that combined with his athletic ability provided him the opportunity to play for Liverpool and earn him his scholarship to the University of San Diego.

With his plan in place, it was time to orchestrate. Michael considered purchasing prefabricated marketing pieces. The major pro of this choice was he could get his site up and running quickly. However, Michael saw significant challenges with these products. He was concerned that the messaging might come across as sounding canned and superficial. Also, in many instances, they weren't exclusive to the purchaser, meaning it could be found elsewhere. If the company did offer territorial protection, it was with a heavy price tag.

Michael made the decision to author all publications sponsored by his website, www.michaeladeery.com, to meet his criterion of keeping his material innovative and fresh. He took to heart this quote from Hockey Hall of Fame's Wayne Gretzsky: "A good hockey player plays where the puck is. A great hockey player plays where the puck is going to be." Michael felt confident he was going in the direction of the future.

Michael tapped into one of his favorite pastimes: reading. He gathered an abundance of data from a multitude of sources. The Internet was his encyclopedia. He used it to search for topics that would interest his existing clientele and potential community of followers. At the same time, Michael made a point of staying on top of current economic and real estate market trends by reading a variety of trade publications. He paid attention to the multitude of program changes and tightening underwriting guidelines, then translated them to a format any reader could easily understand.

Michael's strongest pillar of business came from the consumer. This is whom he catered to in the beginning. Before publishing his work, he went through a filtering process to determine whether what he had learned had merit for his online community. If it did, Michael used the information in his twice-monthly blog. Once he established his rhythm, Michael expanded upon his strategy to encompass the real estate community.

Incorporating the same guiding principles, Michael created *The Mortgage Market Insider*, in 2009. The publication he launched nearly a decade ago is still well received by the real estate professional. Michael refines and tweaks the content from his consumer blog to be appropriate for this monthly newsletter.

2008 was also the year when Michael ventured into the social media arena. Since then, he has enjoyed great success using Facebook, where he posts daily. Michael's ultimate goal with this platform was to build his website subscriber list. At the writing of this book, his business page "Michael Deery & Citywide Financial" boasted almost 7,900 followers. Michael attributes 10 percent of his business today to his Facebook efforts.

Today, he receives 1,500 views on average. To reach a wider audience of individuals who aren't currently following him on his business page, Michael pays to boost his post. Although Facebook offers varied pricing options for increased visibility, Michael hasn't needed to spend more than $10 to $15 at a time. This method of marketing increases his exposure up to 5,000 or more new viewers. He writes about hot topics to drive additional traffic to his website. Boosting his posts has been a key element to getting new buyers and refinances from people who are clicking and reading his material.

REACHING NEW HEIGHTS

By 2009, Michael had spent a year devoting all his efforts to cultivating his image and reaping the rewards from those activities. He decided it was time to capitalize on the momentum he had created.

His blog and newsletter did a good job of keeping him in front of his 11,000+ readership, and prompted them to call when they needed his services; however, the approach was passive. Michael recognized he needed to change this dynamic and become more assertive by instigating the contact. His change in mindset required him to reach out proactively at critical junctures of his clientele's life. Figuring this out became the next major turning point in his career.

In addition to what he was already doing, Michael began sending his clients a copy of their final HUD-1 Settlement Statement. The closing agent prepared this document at the time the transaction consummated. However, most customers misplaced their paperwork. On or about the third week of January in the following year, Michael made a point of resending it to them.

In the present environment, originators have replaced the HUD with the final Closing Disclosure.

This practice was well received, but he didn't stop there. With the assistance of the LoanToolBox™ program, and the customized (Act!) version included in his membership, Michael was able to personalize his marketing even further. Instead of relying on instinct, he scheduled his communication based on the borrower's milestones. Before reaching out, Michael took the time to refresh his memory by reading the last couple of conversations he had documented in the history section of the software. As evidenced by his rising production, Michael has done an amazing job of wrapping his arms around customer retention. Today, more than 50 percent of his clientele are from referrals.

The implementation of his database nearly eight years ago took his production to new heights, and it's still climbing. By 2011, Hallie's workload was intense. Not only was she the sole processor, but she also managed areas of his business that were not processing-specific. Together they decided it made sense to bring on another person. This would enable her to delegate communicating status and the handling of any required follow-up. Nancy Smith, with her accounting background, was exactly who they needed.

Michael decided that writing a weekly column for the local newspaper was just the ticket to increase exposure and elevate his credibility even further than it already was. He connected with the managing editor of *The San Diego Tribune* (now *The San Diego-Union Tribune)* with his desire to write for the paper. To demonstrate the seriousness of his intentions, Michael invited her to subscribe to both his blog and newsletter to check out his writing. It also gave her the chance to validate his skill and commitment. The editor took him up on his offer. What a brilliant strategic way to separate himself from others that had the same idea of approaching the *Tribune*.

Reaching out to the local newspaper is not a foreign idea. It is, however, not often that the green light is granted for a weekly column to someone who is not a journalist. The paper has since gone through three subsequent editors. Each time a new one comes aboard, Michael goes through the same steps with the new person to remain as the paper's subject matter expert. He employs the same approach whenever he requests the opportunity to write for regional, state, and national publications. It works every time.

While Michael acknowledges that it's unlikely that the public consciously thinks, "This person writes for the local newspaper, so he must be credible," the reality is that it's often what they conclude at some level. This is why he still puts a considerable amount of effort into his writing, a highly productive activity that delivers the essence of his vision. To be *the* resource for real estate financing.

LESS IS MORE

Michael Deery is a prime example of someone who stripped his business model down to its simplest format. In his case, initially, it was out of necessity; however, no matter what the driver, you deserve a practice that fits your lifestyle. When Michael had to let twenty-five people go, he could have buried his head in the sand. Michael could have played the victim, blaming the world for a set of circumstances beyond his control. But he didn't do that, rather, he made the decision to create a machine that runs lean and mean. Instead of spreading himself too thin trying to manage others, Michael stayed true to his vision and did not waiver. He looked at the big picture and grew leaps and bounds. Despite what one would expect to happen that first year or two, his income did not drop. Instead, it went in the opposite direction. What kind of personal production numbers are we talking about? Here is what the *Scotsman Guide* has posted for the last six years:

YEAR	RANKING	DOLLAR VOLUME	CLOSED UNITS
2016	173	$115,505,534	272
2015	146	$104,750,885	256
2014	56	$101,450,310	254
2013	133	$92,505,475	245
2012	216	$88,651,465	229
2011	159	$62,000,500	152

Michael's story contains valuable insights. He has built an amazing legacy. He dismantled processes that did not work and continued to refine them until they produced the results he wanted. Never once did he shy away from the tasks that needed handling. Michael continues to operate this way. To summarize his secrets for success:

- **Branding your self-image is extremely important.** You have to know how you want others to see you. How you want them to think about and describe you. Then you need to become bullet proof regarding your written and oral word. Michael wanted recognition as the foremost expert in his field. The postings on his website and social media have fostered the persona and perception that he envisioned in those dark days of 2008. The articles he's written for local, regional, and national publications adds further to his credentials.

- **Pro-active, diligent communications are essential ingredients to maintain relationships.** From the time that first introduction occurs, or the consumer generates an inquiry, until long after the loan consummates, it's vital to create top of mind awareness. Starting out strong and ending on a weak note causes as much, if not more, damage. There will be times that tough calls may need to happen and, when they do putting them off does not serve any one.

- **Lead generation is a constant activity and is not reserved for only rookies.** For those initially getting into the lending industry, a considerable amount of time spent cold calling is required. Waiting for the phone to ring will not put food on the table. If people want to build a prosperous sales careers, they need customers. Good old-fashioned dialing is a great way to start. And those with an established customer base can easily lose traction if they become too complacent to pick up their phone.

Michael's future just keeps getting brighter and brighter. He and his beautiful wife, Danielle, welcomed their second child, Conor, who joins his sister, three-year-old Keira Annabella. The family travels back to Ireland at least once a year where Michael reacquaints himself with the land that helped shape him. His quest for never-ending improvement has provided a business model that not only works, but one that he enjoys day in and day out. Who would have thought the worst days of someone's life could lead them to a place beyond their wildest imagination?

TEACH, ADAPT, LEARN: BE TAL!

Told to and shared by Cindy

———❈———

There may be people that have more talent than you, but there's no
excuse for anyone to work harder than you do.

—DEREK JETER

TIMELINE	EMPLOYER	ROLE
During the 2007–2008 Financial Crisis	Wellington Financial Group	Broker/Owner
Present Employer 2017	Waterstone Mortgage Corp.	Branch Manager

MIKE SMALLEY entered real estate lending in 2002, right after graduating
with a finance degree from Florida State University. At that time, not only
was the economy horrendous, he lacked experience. It made finding a
job in his field very difficult. Mike had a friend, who worked for a staffing
agency. She knew of a company that would hire loan officers without any
prior experience. They offered both commercial and residential lending.
From the sound of what his friend described, Mike felt he had the qualifications to meet the job requirements.

Originally, he thought the commercial division would be the best fit for him. However, within the first sixty days, he realized that was not the direction he wanted to head. He moved over to the residential side of the business, and knew immediately he'd found his calling. Mike remained there a little more than a year before opening his own brokerage shop, Wellington Financial Group, in 2004.

His employer didn't offer on-the-job training, which wasn't uncommon in the mortgage industry during that time frame. To educate himself, Mike subscribed to several trade publications, and attended as many sales-focused events and industry related conferences as possible. One of the most influential seminars he attended was Tim Braheem's Business Plan 2006. Tim stressed the importance of being knowledgeable. He contended the reason originators suffered from call reluctance was because they were not confident in their level of expertise. Tim delved further saying that having a stellar presentation was of the utmost importance. He advocated practice, practice, practice until the salesperson's script was bulletproof. Tim felt following these recommendations is what prepared individuals to have the skills necessary to counter sales objections when they came-up. He also promoted the importance of systems, and shared his 72-step plan to perfect the loan process with participants. Mike definitely could relate to everything he heard.

SWEPT UP IN A HOUSING BUBBLE

On top of having to learn a new profession, Mike had market conditions to contend with. In the early 2000s, the real estate market in Florida was just joining the housing bubble that had already swept various parts of the nation. This was confirmed when the Office of Federal Housing Enterprise Oversight (OFHEO) performed their analysis on the Orlando housing market[1]. The report was prepared with the guidance and assistance of the Housing and Urban Development's Economic and Market Analysis Division. Their findings indicated that home prices in April 2003 exceeded what consumers had for disposable income. The report confirmed what Mike already knew.

Another indicator of the housing bubble in the area Mike serviced were the lotteries builders held. New construction had been on the rise, and normally this would be a good thing. However, demand was *so* high that builders were able to flip the lots they had for sale two to three times, for considerable increases each time, contributing to the bloated prices. When a bubble is not present, home values typically rise at the pace of inflation plus one or two percentage points. Orlando had far surpassed that. This situation would continue at full speed over the next five years. On September 20, 2006, the Legislative Office of Economic and Demographic Research cited the following statistics:

- Median house prices soared 90 percent from July 2001 to July 2006.

- Housing boom lasted five years, but began to decline in 2005.

- Statewide sales dropped 33 percent.[2]

Mike's average loan size reflected an even higher increase than what is illustrated above. In 2002, his average loan amount was $150,000 jumping to $300,000 in 2006. It would not stabilize until several years later. As of this writing, his average loan size is at $250,000.

The aforementioned report also stated that 30 percent of the loans written were exotic and subprime loans. These included the No Income No Asset (NINA) products that didn't require any validation of a borrower's qualifications. Stated Income Stated Asset (SISA) loans were also popular. As the name implies, the customer stated their earnings and bank balance. During the first half of the decade, pretty much anyone who was alive and breathing could get a loan from a hefty selection of companies.

Though the report included subprime mortgages in their assessment, it's important to recognize that not all subprime loans are considered to be predatory in nature. If the creditor determines that the borrower has the ability to repay the mortgage, it no longer falls under the predatory category. There are times when people feel it's worth taking a loan with higher a rate and fees. They would rather buy now instead of having to wait until they meet the standard qualifications for conforming underwriting guidelines. Borrowers who do not have enough seasoning since their bankruptcy or foreclosure is one example. Properties that don't conform to the local zoning codes are another instance where subprime loans serve a purpose.

The issue the Consumer Financial Protection Bureau (CFPB) has with loan products that have exotic features, as a general statement, is the creditor typically isn't concerned whether or not the borrower can make the payment. This is because all of the weight is placed on the equity the property contains. Mike Smalley definitely wanted to avoid those types of mortgage products.

At the time of our interview, Mike said when he first started in the industry there was an abundance of tax shelter schemes and shell corporations being created to avoid paying taxes. Fraud ran rampant in the territory he was calling on. Mike heard about numerous transactions where straw buyers were involved. This occurs when a person purchases a home in their name on behalf of another person without disclosing that fact to the lender, making the transaction fraudulent. The ramification of multiple sales to straw buyers is it creates fictitious or pie in the sky equity. Houses that sold at $400,000 three to six months earlier now had an inflated value of $500,000 after being flipped several times. Mike said it was like the wild, wild, west.

SHARING CORE VALUES

This was an incredibly difficult time for law-abiding loan officers to make a living. Marketing Service Agreements (MSAs) were also common occurrence in Mike's marketplace. An MSA is a contract between two parties where one party agrees to pay a fee to the other party for their marketing efforts. The CFPB has concern in this area, as the arrangement may be masking an inducement for business, which results in the consumer paying higher fees for settlement provider services. If this is the case, it is a direct violation of Section 8 of the Real Estate Settlement Providers Act (RESPA). Typically, this arrangement involves the real estate broker or builder and a lender or a title company. During 2004 (up until Dodd-Frank went into effect), Mike was competing heavily against lenders who paid to have a desk space within the broker/builder location. In some instances, as much as $15,000 a month.

In his early days, he also faced pressure from another direction. With the broker's blessing in some cases, agents would not refer business to a loan officer unless they were willing to pay them a portion of their commission—

a definite RESPA violation. This wasn't something Mike was willing to do. As far as he was concerned, even if the law didn't prohibit him from giving up part of his commission for services not rendered, Mike saw no reason to devalue himself or the service he provides. While he stayed true to himself, the culture was tough. I asked Mike if he'd thought about leaving the profession with what he was facing. "No, I didn't," he said. "I was still earning good money and I felt confident my reputation would prevail eventually."

Mike certainly could have thrown in the towel, but instead, he offered only clean alternatives. This was his way of dealing with the corruption he was witnessing around him. Mike was bound and determined to find and work with people with similar values, morals, and ethics. And guess what? He found them.

LUNCH AND LEARN

In 2006, Mike added Lunch and Learns to his repertoire. For the first few years he held these meetings weekly. The sessions run from thirty to sixty minutes. This strategy gave him the ability to get in front of a group of influencers all at once. Initially there were about forty to fifty people who attended. They left with the tools to sell at least one more home, which in turn gave them the opportunity to make more money. Talk about giving people a reason to be pumped up. And of course, if Mike wasn't already their lender of choice, he was surely on the right track to earning their business. From experience, he has learned keeping the meeting size at ten to twenty creates a more intimate atmosphere. Since Mike can spend more time interacting he is able to establish a rapport much sooner with individuals with whom he doesn't have an existing relationship.

At the onset, Mike didn't want his guests to be distracted or motivated by anything other than the message he was presenting. He kept the refreshments and the room simple, to deter those who'd just come for the free food with no intention of sending clients his way. Why would he want their participation? The answer was he did not. Mike's philosophy on this is spot on. People most often rate an event's success by the number of people who show up rather than by the actual business generated from their efforts.

One of the topics Mike covered included selling homes that had issues—such as old roofs, dilapidated pools, or subpar electrical wiring—using the 203K mortgage as a financing option. In these instances, the repairs are completed after closing. Often these properties were difficult to market. The program benefited both the buyer and the seller. The borrowers knew they had the funding necessary and the owners could sell the home without doing the work. Mike also covered a slew of other relevant topics, including those related to unmarketable title, the up and coming programs, as well as ways to improve sales techniques. Many of his sessions include a co-presenter, which further benefits the attendees, and reduces Mike's costs proportionately, because they share in the expenses.

Mike was able to accomplish several objectives with his Lunch and Learns. The audience viewed the speaker (in this case, him) as knowledgeable and an expert in his field (which he is.) It elevated his status improving the quality of his referrals dramatically. Following the same format, Mike also has meetings with individual agent teams. Everything remains the same, including the material he presents; the only differential is the group size, which runs between four and six.

Six to eight years ago, he started sponsoring a mastermind group for real estate agents. Mike got the idea from his own involvement in one that he was a part of with other loan officers. He's derived great benefits from his participation. Since it continues to be a good experience for him, he figured it would be of value for his agents. Currently, there are five members in his agent mastermind group. These are Mike's top echelon. They meet over lunch to share ideas and brainstorm on a monthly basis. As his business has grown, and with the addition of team meetings and the mastermind group he hosts, Mike has reduced the frequency of his Lunch and Learns to once a month.

BUILDING A STRONG CUSTOMER BASE

One of the key elements of Mike's strategy from the beginning was to collect business cards during these sessions. After speaking with someone, he wrote brief notes on the back. Mike also listed any suggestions they gave to him, along with any referrals he received so he could properly thank them. Once Mike returned to the office, he entered the data in his CRM. Most importantly, Mike followed up with everyone—not just a quick e-mail, but an old-fashioned handwritten note. He's still following up today. And yes, Mike still collects cards if the agent is new to the broker's office. The only difference between 2006 and now is that Mike has three assistants to help him manage his robust practice.

In the beginning of his career, Mike didn't have a customer base to draw from, which is the case for many new loan originators. Instead of waiting for transactions to land at his feet, he tapped into a resource rich with people who loved and respected him. Mike created a list of family members, friends he grew up with, went to school with, and played sports with in high school, college, and professionally to jump-start his business. Mike calls this his wedding theory: if he would invite the individual to his large wedding, he put their name down. Mike reached out to every single person on the list to let them know he was in the business to provide mortgage financing, and that he was the one they needed to reach out to and *not* someone else.

Besides creating an effective method of building his business, Mike improved his communication skills with each call he made and every meeting he held. His perseverance paid off. Mike became increasingly successful at converting his leads into active deals that consummated. Once the transaction closed, Mike asked his borrowers to introduce him to their family, friends and co-workers who also needed his services. The beauty of his strategy was that it didn't cost him a single penny. However, it did require time and effort. It also required Mike to have focus and discipline, both of which he tapped into while playing college and professional baseball.

Mike had previously been an all-star standout for Bishop Moore High School. His talent as a pitcher landed him a scholarship to Florida State University (FSU). The month he graduated high school, the Pittsburgh Pirates drafted him in the twenty-third round. When asked how it made him feel, Mike said he felt his "hard work had paid off."

Although tempted, he turned down the offer to play professional baseball because he wanted to have the college experience. However, at the end of his junior year at (FSU), the Atlanta Braves came knocking on his door. Once again, Mike was picked in the twenty-third round of the Amateur Draft. This time he decided to play. He stayed with the team for two years before returning to school to get his finance degree. Injuries, burnout, and the desire to enter the real world prompted that decision. Today, Mike coaches the youth in his town of Winter Park, Florida. His players went to Cooperstown and won it all in 2016. This winning spirit coupled with successful outcomes follows him today. The saying "practice makes perfect" was and is something he buys into 100 percent. Mike knows he can't stop there, though. It's just not enough to be better than others, you also have to be able to stand out from the crowd.

One of the observations Mike made early on in his career was that the people he competed with tended to be transaction-focused. For the most part, they would complete one deal and then move on to the next. He realized that if he wanted to grow exponentially, he needed to increase his sphere of influence in the broker community. In his opinion, the fastest way to accomplish that goal was to have his clients endorse him to their real estate professionals. He found the best time to ask for a warm reference is when customers are happy and completely satisfied.

To ensure this was the case, Mike began taking a pulse, usually halfway through the process, to make sure that all parties felt good about their experience. If they weren't the team worked on getting the issue resolved immediately.

If everyone was pleased, Mike felt he had earned the right to request his borrower's recommendation. Next, he'd schedule a one-on-one meeting with the real estate professional. The purpose was to see if he felt a connection and find out if they had the same moral compass as he did. If there was a values match, then there was a basis to work together. This strategy in combination with the other things he had implemented worked well for him, and within a few years of his career, Mike was able to build a loyal following of agents.

LEARN, ADAPT, INCORPORATE, AND GO

In 2006, the effects of the mortage crisis were starting to be felt. While other lenders were eliminating products, leaving the market, or abandoning their clientele, Mike and his team zoomed in. He worked long hours securing new clients and saving the deals his former competitors had left behind, building up his database in the process. While others needed to advertise that they were still in the business, had changed companies or still continued to offer product X, Y, or Z, to get customers, Mike did not need to do any of that. He got referral, after referral, after referral from his agents and closed customer base. Staying committed to working with people who shared his morals and ethics has paid off big time.

Mike was very cognizant that change was in the wind. As the financial crisis was in full swing, the regulations created tougher underwriting guidelines. The steps required to remain compliant increased, intruding on his origination time. He investigated the merits of changing his status from being a broker owner to working for a mortgage banker. After deciding this is what would be best for him, Mike began the interviewing process.

In 2008, Mike made the decision to join Waterstone Mortgage Corp., as a branch. While he did give up some of his autonomy and control, the net branch model lifted a lot of responsibility from his shoulders. It eliminated a number of day-to-day of issues he had needed to deal with as a broker-owner, subsequently easing a lot of his workload and worry. The best part was he could focus on originating loans. Mike's philosophy is people can either sing the blues or they can accept that there are times when they have no control over change. Sometimes, instead of bellyaching, people just need to keep moving forward. It's a common attitude we've seen among athletes: Greg Frost, Drew McKenzie, and Michael Deery, to name a few. However, as evidenced by the others we have featured before and after this chapter, being athletic is not a pre-requisite to possessing this drive.

Mike continues to stay focused on the purchase market as his primary source of business. Unlike many of his competitors, he didn't rely on refinances to be his bread and butter. Mike shares the same opinion as Drew McKenzie on this point—these transactions are how his clientele reward him for a job well done previously. Mike's attitude, along with his persistence, and laser focus saved him during the mortgage crisis.

He still places a high emphasis on learning. Mike became involved with The CORE Training, Inc., in 2013, a coaching program that recommends following a strict regimen that has proven to increase production and effi-ciencies for individuals who have the discipline to follow the program. He still attends the annual meeting each year. Why? Because Mike credits the coaching he has received for his significant growth in the past few years. When asked what has been the main benefit to him, Mike said the CORE taught him how to hire and train his people.

Mike shared that when he first started bringing staff on, he found he was too busy, and as a result, he didn't invest the necessary time to train his peo-ple the right way. Things fell through the cracks. The CORE made him realize what was happening. By not dedicating adequate time he was creating more work for himself, instead of increasing his capacity. Mike had to take a step back to make sure his new hires were trained correctly. In the long run this has saved him time and money. Now there is a procedure in place that the employee who's being promoted or leaving has to follow before their replace-ment takes over. This one change has played an instrumental role in taking his business to a much higher level. But that's not all Mike got from the CORE.

Another idea he got from his coaching was to host a monthly happy hour for real estate, insurance, and title agents. The event typically lasts for an hour and a half. The group size varies between five and fifteen. It gives Mike and the team a chance to mingle and relate on a more personal level with those who attend. Let's take a moment to summarize how Mike built his business from the ground up, while surviving the worst financial crisis since the Depression, and differentiated himself from the competition:

- **Build a list of everyone who cares about you,** because they're the most likely to use your services and recommend you—family, friends, and any one you know from extracurricular activities such as the gym, your place of worship, and little league games, just to name a few. These are the people with whom you have the strongest chemistry.

- **Next bring on the B team**—extended family, friends of friends, col-leagues of colleagues, anyone who knows you without prodding. This is exactly what Mike did in his early years. You'll be amazed at how many people you know.

- **Decide what you want to be known for,** and then make sure to pepper your conversation with these adjectives. There is no right or wrong answer; however, if you are not clear on why someone should work with you, they won't be either. In Mike's case he wanted to be recognized as an expert in his field with a high level of integrity. Some might prefer to have the reputation of a trusted advisor. Still others want to be seen as the top producer or . . . If you're unsure, ask those closest to you to describe you in three to five words. Very quickly, a pattern will begin to emerge. This is what makes you special, why people should and will want to work with you.

- **Before picking up the phone, know your objective.** This is where a majority of salespeople struggle. They do not know what they are trying to achieve, so they do not clearly state their call-to-action. Decide if your goal is to:

  - Ask for business
  - Ask for an endorsement
  - Ask for a referral

Next, *and* most important, start reaching out to these people. The list will not do you any good if it is ignored.

- **Maximize your time by getting in front of a *group* of people.** In addition to his Lunch and Learns, team meetings and mastermind events that he holds, Mike has become a nationally recognized speaker. He has been featured at various mortgage industry events, including Mortgage Revolution, Sales Mastery,™ and Mortgage Mastermind.

- **Don't be afraid to swipe and adapt.** It's not important to reinvent the wheel, just latch onto a proven strategy, then take the time to tweak and refine *until* you have a plan that works for you. Next, implement that plan. The defining difference between those who succeed, and those who do not is implementation.

Today, Mike and his two business partners manage nine regional branches across the state of Florida, with offices in Winter Park, Port Orange, Palm Coast, Panama City, Ft. Walton Beach, Niceville, Ocala, Ft. Myers, and Jupiter. He's actively originating, earning President's Club status each year since joining Waterstone Mortgage with the help of his closed clients and agent referrals. His personal production is in the neighborhood of $60 million a year, which equates to twenty closings a month. The branch he oversees closes $600 million in production annually. He's able to keep his workweek at forty-five hours while managing forty-five loan officers in his region. Sticking to his moral compass, offering clean alternatives has paid off in a big way. It's a home run for sure!

MIRACLES IN MORTGAGE LEADERSHIP: THE ART OF COACHING AND PROVIDING SUPPORT

Told to and shared by Kathleen

———————◆※◆———————

Miracles occur naturally as expressions of love. They are performed by those who temporarily have more for those who temporarily have less.

—ANONYMOUS, AS QUOTED IN *A COURSE IN MIRACLES* BY DR. HELEN SHUCMAN AND WILLIAM THETFORD

TIMELINE	EMPLOYER	ROLE
During the 2007–2008 Financial Crisis	American Home Mortgage	Regional VP
2016	Prospect Mortgage, LLC	Division President South Atlantic
2017	Retired	—

RALPH MASSELLA creates miracles. Before we tell you how, here's a little background. More years ago than he would like to remember, Ralph graduated from the University of Baltimore with a degree in business administration and an emphasis on human resources. After a brief encounter with the reality of the job market in his chosen field in the early '70s, he stumbled into sales. Ralph began his professional career selling life insurance, which later morphed into a position as a debit agent. With his insurance license fresh in hand, the proverbial slap in the face came swiftly, when Ralph's manager handed him a phone book and said, "Here. These are all your potential clients." In 1974, he transitioned to annuities and mortgage insurance sales.

It was hardly ideal, but Ralph dove in. Within a few years, he had developed a sizeable client base, but that didn't go hand-in-hand with an equivalently large paycheck. According to Ralph, his earning potential was capped at $45,000 annually. His brother Michael, who was working in the mortgage industry, had a different reality. During a family get-together, while they were catching up, the conversation segued to how things were going. Ralph shared that he was working a ton of hours for what he considered to be nominal pay. Michael suggested that his brother might want to consider a career in mortgage sales; he then proceeded to whip out his year-end paystub. He had earned a little over $150,000. After seeing that, it didn't take Ralph long to execute a career change. As far as he was concerned, being a mortgage loan officer came as close to self-employment as a person could get without taking on the risks. This held a huge attraction for Ralph. He could continue earning one-third of what his brother was making, or he could take control of his destiny and make a switch. And at the end of 1976, Ralph did exactly that.

His training in the mortgage business was minimal, by anyone's standards. Ralph's boss, Charlie, drove him around, pointing out every real estate office in town. He instructed Ralph that the staff members in these offices were his customer base and he needed to get in front of them. This is a far cry from the educational requirements of today's loan originator, which includes twenty hours of education from an accredited NMLS course, and passing the Uniform State Test. In addition, there is an application fee that is significantly higher for those who don't work for a depository institution.

Schooling from Charlie, however, did include invaluable life lessons. For example, Ralph was about one week into his new job when his boss asked him to deliver a box of mortgage financing guides to a local real estate office on Capitol Hill. Ralph told Charlie that based on his limited knowledge and training, he did not feel ready to start talking to a room full of agents. "Ralph," Charlie said, "Just hand them to the receptionist. She is expecting you. Then return to the office."

He took the box of finance guides and did as instructed. When Ralph arrived, the receptionist greeted him warmly and told him that everyone was looking forward to hearing what he had to share. "I'm just supposed to give these guides to you," he said, but she ignored his comment as she led him down the hallway.

When Ralph entered he saw there were about twenty agents sitting in classroom style seating. The broker came up to him with a big smile and proclaimed to the group, "Ralph from Hamilton Mortgage is here to give us some FHA financing training!" Perspiration created an immediate "glow" on his face while he stood there, frozen. Ralph asked to use the phone before getting started. Then he proceeded to call his boss and explain the situation. Charlie just laughed and instructed Ralph to go for it. He also reminded him of Rule #1: When you don't know the answer just say, "Give me a few minutes to find out, and I'll get right back to you." That rule stuck with Ralph his whole career: Do not bluff. You cannot know everything. Always tell the truth. After hanging up, Ralph went back into the room, stood up in front of the group and asked everyone to open the materials he'd brought. Then Ralph began: "The FHA program was founded in 1934 by Franklin Delano Roosevelt," and he went on from there.

Ralph said he learned several things that day, both in general and about himself. Stuff that individuals have to experience firsthand. Going through these types of experiences reveals much about who you *are*, and the work required to reach the potential of who you want *to be*. Charlie was very wise putting Ralph through what he initially considered a terrifying ordeal early on in his career. It forced him to trust himself to do the job, and to have the confidence in his abilities. They worked together for more than twenty years becoming lifelong friends. Sadly, Charlie has since passed away.

From that day forward, Ralph got over his initial fears, and began to call on real estate offices. He knew if he wanted to gain market share he had to show up on a regular basis *and* he had to be readily available to whomever was reaching out to him. Ralph remembers the days before cell phones, the days of pagers and using pay phones at gas stations to return those pages. He always took the time to pull off the road and return calls promptly. This simple strategy was what set him apart from his competition. Ralph's communication went beyond what his clients expected and what they received from others. It wasn't long before he exceeded his company's minimum of thirty closings a month. At that time, there wasn't much tolerance for people who didn't produce a significant loan volume; in fact, termination happened swiftly. Ralph was certainly aware of this, and rather than losing his job, he chose to do the hard work.

HUMANITARIAN AND EDUCATOR

Ralph's first year in the business was the same year that the Community Reinvestment Act (CRA) was passed by the 95th Congress. President Jimmy Carter had signed it in to law shortly thereafter. The enactment of this regulation bears mentioning because it affects the course of lending even now. The purpose of the act was to address what the government perceived as discrimination toward individuals and businesses in low- and moderate-income neighborhoods. It encouraged banking institutions to help meet the credit needs of what the regulators considered to be underserved communities. The law affects any entities that fall under the Federal Deposit Insurance Corporation's (FDIC) jurisdiction. They must adhere to the requirements of the directive by loaning a percentage of their funds at reduced rates and fees.

To offset the lower revenue CRA loans generated, banks and commercial lenders began to promote adjustable rate mortgages. Consumers qualified at the initial start, or "teaser," rate to help them obtain a higher mortgage amount. However, the challenge was that some people who chose an ARM were ill-prepared once the adjustment period began to take effect and their payment increased.

The Graduated Payment Mortgage (GPM) was another alternative conceived. In this case, payments started out even lower than the ARM. What was nice about this loan product was that the payment didn't adjust. Borrowers could choose to pay the fully amortized amount or pay the minimum and have the unpaid interest added to their existing balance. The latter is what caused the loan to have negative amortization. In the case of both the ARM and the GPM, new homeowners were attracted to the lower payments, since they tended to be more in line with what they were used to spending for rent, thereby reducing potential payment shock. Many thought their homes would appreciate at the same rate or even faster than the accruing interest. Unfortunately, this was not always the case.

Ralph wisely knew he needed a different alternative for borrowers who were attracted to ARMS and GPMs. As rates began to climb in the early '80s, Ralph promoted FHA and VA financing by upping the frequency of the seminars he held in the brokers' offices. These loans had less restrictive qualifying guidelines and were also an excellent option for individuals that had minimal funds to work with. During these workshops it was common for Ralph to receive a standing ovation from those in attendance. Sometimes they started clapping when he first entered the room. Why? Because instead of talking *at* them with the standard sales spin, Ralph was working *with* them. He took the time to educate them on how to increase sales and earn more money while providing an alternative that was in the best interest of their clients.

In 1994, during a slow period at his current employer Waterfield Mortgage, Ralph looked for innovative ways to help his originators market themselves. Since the competition could be fierce, he felt his agents had to differentiate themselves. Ralph noticed that top-producing listing agents shared a common thread. They took the time to build a strong presentation prior to meeting with a prospective seller. They prepared a customized packet that illustrated why they were the best choice. It included how the agent was going to market the property, as well as how they arrived at the recommended list price. It also contained customer testimonials that attested to high satisfaction levels with their services.

Ralph realized his salespeople faced virtually the same challenge of proving their worthiness to real estate agents and the other professional partners they wanted to work with. He designed a presentation book that followed a similar format as the one listing agents used. At first, the material centered on promoting the company. As time went on, however, it included more about the loan officer, their experience, and accomplishments. Testimonials from borrowers and professional partners who worked with them were included as well. Ralph didn't stop there.

He started working on a program he called Tractivities. The concept behind his data-driven productivity system was to improve sales skills. Using the goals originators set for themselves, he built algorithms to measure the results their activities produced. Ralph felt that for salespeople to be in alignment with their desires, they must go through a self-realization/self-awareness process. Tractivities provided a dashboard that measured performance in real time. He beta tested the program on loan officers who reported to him.

In 1995, when Ralph left Waterfield to accept employment with Columbia National, he presented Tractivities to the executives. Ralph hoped his new company would see the value of what he was working on, and they most certainly did. They loved the idea. Columbia wanted to take the program to another level by making it Palm Pilot-compatible. The Palm was considered to be one of the newest and coolest technologies of 1996. The executives decided to rebrand the name to Sales Emphasis Training, or SET. They felt the system went beyond tracking an originator's activities; it enabled them to soar.

Here is how SET worked. Loan officers entered data into their handheld device. The information was uploaded to the company server almost instantaneously. Before long, salespeople started securing an increased number of qualified prospects that led to more closings. Why was that? Because seeing which actions paid off motivated them. Ralph recognized that for an individual to buy in to doing the right things they couldn't feel strapped to a system that pigeonholed them. The genius in Ralph's program is that it relied on the individual's definition of personal success. An unexpected but *very* welcome benefit was that it tipped the scales when recruiting top-producing loan officers. They loved it! This was big.

American Home Mortgage (AHM) acquired Columbia National in 2001. Ralph stayed on because he was impressed with the company's dedication to technology. Once again, the executive team liked what they saw and gave him the green light to further develop the program. Ralph's brainchild underwent another name change to Work Initiatives Now (WIN). Instead of building it out on his own, he formed a team of the best and brightest people from various departments including Operations, IT, and Finance. In some cases, he facilitated the hiring of new top people to assist with gap analysis, and to provide feedback that would influence the design of the WIN system.

WHY HIM?

The CEO and founder of AHM wanted to accelerate the organization's growth. I had a reputation for doing exactly that. I joined the company in 2003. I immediately noticed a companywide lack of reporting and technology tools. When I questioned the CEO about this he directed me to Ralph, who had joined AHM two years before. I recall thinking, *Ralph Massella. Why him? He's one of the company's top regional VPs. I don't get it.* I soon did.

During our first meeting, it was clear to me that Ralph had noticed the same gaps I had. Here's what I loved about what he had rolled out to the loan officers under his purview. I knew, as did Ralph, that salespeople who scheduled intentional meetings instead of just showing up won big. And not just any meeting, but those that involved partnership planning sessions with real estate agents, builders, financial planners or other professional partners. Conducting pre-approvals with clients also fell into this category. Ralph's program was proving what we both already knew, and the numbers in his region reflected that. I shared my feedback with the CEO. This gave Ralph the increased authority and funding he needed to build out WIN on a much grander scale, so all members of the sales team companywide could benefit.

Ralph's team was *on* it. In a few short years, our technology and reporting systems were the best in the industry and getting better every day. The WIN dashboard progressed to reflect which lead sources resulted in the highest conversion to closed loans. The underlying fundamental of submitting a complete file and setting realistic expectations instead of having to backpedal on broken promises enhanced the agent's business model and reputation. The brilliance of what Ralph created, and his desire to constantly improve, proved again and again to be a winning solution.

Even though Ralph is an early serial adopter of new technology, he believes it's still vital to be responsive to phone calls, texts, and requests for in-person meetings. Ralph isn't a huge believer in e-mail or voicemail; he feels both depersonalize relationships. So why would Ralph, a guy who was responsible for sales in a huge geographical region do so much work in an area that didn't directly concern him? Because Ralph has always taken action rather than sitting on the sidelines.

Some may wonder if Ralph ultimately dropped out of the team and let the others take over. He never did. His motivation stemmed from face-to-face, one-on-one interactions with his team leaders, his loan officers, and his operations staff. He sees life as a giant puzzle that has to be put together. With every missing piece he finds, he begins to create, hire, implement, and so on, until all the pieces fit together. This process translates down to the loan officer level beautifully. Ralph is a marathon kind of person; he thinks sprints are for lightweights. And yes, he actually does run marathons and just completed his latest one in September 2017.

There will always be something happening in the marketplace that affects a person's growth. For those who do not have a thriving mortgage practice, blaming changing conditions might provide a very convenient excuse for their lack of success. Not for Ralph. In addition to the forces he could not control professionally, Ralph has faced tragedies that many would find to be debilitating, painful, and even completely life-altering. He has found a way to use every one of those experiences to pay it forward with his kindness and mentorship.

Ralph's son Damien died in 1998 at the age of seventeen from a heroin overdose. The circumstances surrounding his son's death left many unanswered questions. Recognizing that others, too, went through a difficult time in these terrible situations, Ralph and his family established Damien's Run for Recovery and Damien's Recovery.

Damien's Run for Recovery had their 19th annual 5K run on June 4, 2017. Each year, all the proceeds from this event have gone to not-for-profit organizations such as Damien's Recovery, Inc. The race has provided a public forum that has garnished a lot of community support and gone a long way to remove the stigma associated with addiction.

Damien's Recovery has been working with Howard County Drug Free, a local government agency to raise awareness in schools. They offer scholarships to college-bound students who are independent of financial aid and are planning to engage in one of the following areas of course study: education, social work, counseling, outdoor education, or any other area involving young people. That way, those who currently *have more* will eventually assist those who temporarily *have less*.

What Ralph didn't do was to let circumstances hold him back. This is a critical point. The majority of top producers Cindy and I have worked with have that same commonality. They never play the excuse game. In what way does this quality transfer over to mortgage leadership? In our opinion, in every way.

Ralph focuses on having people transcend from their comfort zone and move into their genius zone. He helps them to do that by being conscious of their mindset. It enables individuals to have an understanding of what they need to do to succeed. They also need to comprehend the rules of engagement. Further, there has to be an understanding of psychology. This comes into play when dealing with people, and it's integral to the entire sales dynamic.

When asked why he believes productivity results are lower today, Ralph said in his opinion there are several factors: "Today's salespeople have two mentalities that are polar opposites. For some of them, being a loan officer is a part-time job. Others have a stockbroker approach. They only want the juicy loans with a large commission. They think the others are not worth their time." He disagrees with both perceptions.

When Ralph was a loan officer, he developed processes and activities to determine where he could best source his business from, and, as a manager, he incorporated what he had learned about people from his previous experiences. Ralph knew without a doubt there was a correlation between success and those who had a passion for what the job entailed. Without this combination, chances were an individual would only perform at mediocre levels. Additionally, he noted that talented people are hired for the wrong position far too frequently. Ralph employed these realizations and other strategies to build the best sales teams in his power during his tenure at AHM, and later at Bank of America and Prospect Mortgage, LLC, until he retired in 2016.

- **Hire only the right people with the right skills, goals, temperament, and focus.** Ralph was particular about who he recruited, and subsequently brought on board. He understands it might be tempting to hire your sister's best friend who is a top manager for a competitor. However, if you know his/her activities and beliefs don't fit with yours, you'd be better off hiring a bartender with the right drive, desire, and core values, then training him/her on the specifics.

- **Train managers to lead, and help them do that.** Ralph believed in off-site retreats. Using the time away from the office allowed him to emphasize education, focus, and the importance of driving the right activities. Participants were not distracted with day-to-day interruptions. These retreats were also great fun and helped build teams better than almost any other method used to accomplish the same thing.

- **Roll up your sleeves and walk the walk.** Ralph encouraged his managers to go on sales calls with loan officers. They could witness the interaction firsthand, and also have the opportunity to meet with their brokers, real estate agents, builders, financial planners, and so on to hear feedback. Ralph followed this same philosophy of having boots on the ground his entire lending career.

- **Know your customer and their needs.** As a regional VP, Ralph knew his primary customer was his managerial/leadership team. Just as they knew their main priority was the production and operations staff who made up the organization. Operations understood that the branches were their main customer. The support team in the branch had sales as their chief focus. Loan officers concentrated their efforts toward their professional partners and borrowers.

- ◆ **Identify people with high drive and aspirations.** Ralph looked for people who had a desire to grow and a willingness to get past their own self-imposed obstacles, which might prevent them from reaching their full potential. The only way to find these individuals is to ask questions. Here are some that Ralph recommends:

  - What are your specific short- and long-term goals?
  - How many hours do you work each day?
  - Does your family support the number of hours you work?
  - What is one silly thing you did recently?
  - What motivates you?
  - How skilled are you in technology?
  - Do you or will you love what is required of you in this position?
  - When you get to a fork in the road, which way do you go and why?
  - What fulfills you?
  - How would your family and friends describe you?
  - Describe your ideal career path.
  - What steps are you willing to take to achieve your career goals?
  - Are you a ROAR person (one with responsibility, organization skills, accountability, and relationship-building excellence)?
  - What are your boundaries?
  - What does a closed door mean to you and how do you open it?
  - Describe the role of your operations team. Do you see them as partners and why?
  - Do you believe you can bring what you love into your work? Give me an example of that.
  - Is your business life also part of your social experience?
  - What things do you hope to learn about your clients, the business, yourself?
  - How do you positively affect other people?

- With whom do you have relationships that are in your comfort zone?

♦ **Invest in relationships.** Ralph recommends spending at least 20 percent of your workweek interacting with your team. It's worth the time it takes to ask open-ended questions and listen to what they tell you. Encourage your team to come to you with their challenges and then answer them honestly. Investing this time will be well worth it because it strengthens the bond you have over time, so that when roadblocks occur, and they will, you will all get past them. It is also what is instrumental in building loyalty.

TURBULENT TIMES

We've demonstrated that Ralph Massella has focus and is very methodical. He has the mindset to succeed. It's a part of his internal DNA, and it's what drives him to help others. But even Ralph's systems couldn't help him navigate the mortgage meltdown as smoothly as he would have liked. I call this Ralph's Phoenix period.

When it was clear in July 2007 that AHM would be declaring bankruptcy, we shifted into "finding a new home" phase for our sales force. By this time, Ralph and two others had received promotions to senior regional positions based on their volume and leadership skills. (As a side note, Ralph and his like-minded cohorts preferred the title Super Regionals. This was evidenced by the full Superman regalia Ralph donned for that small group at a national sales rally.

Ralph, I, and the other members of the executive team had entered into the Seven Stages of Grief process: shock/denial, pain/guilt, anger, depression, upward turn, reconstruction, and acceptance/hope. When he first met with some of his suitors, Ralph was in the anger phase, and we heard all about it. That quickly passed, however, and he soon found the first of what he thought was a home for himself and many of his team members.

The new company, one of the big box banks, turned out to only be a temporary shelter. Unfortunately, it wasn't the right culture fit for them. Ralph and his group were on track to close an astounding $8 billion (yes, that is with a B) before management decided to split his territory for no rational reason. So he looked for work elsewhere.

No one realized the scope of the mortgage crisis when it started. We all thought finding a new company to work for would be a snap. We planned to take as many of our former co-workers with us as possible. That turned out to just not be the case. For example, many AHM employees ended up going to Indy Mac or Countrywide. But before long, neither of those companies existed.

Fear and mistrust comprised public sentiment about mortgage lenders and banks in general during the years of the Great Recession, lingering for the next several years. The words, "Trust us, we're too big to fail," quickly rang shallow and false. Many peers and direct reports who vowed to work with you again at a new company ended up negotiating deals for themselves only. They even occasionally built walls to ensure that their so-called friend could not, and would not, be hired. It seems ludicrous, but that's what fear does; it prompts inconceivable behavior.

The compensation packages often didn't materialized. Many top people eventually waved the white flag and left the business. Others desperately accepted different, lower, or unrelated positions in what remained of the mortgage industry at that time. But Ralph, with his hope intact, and a significant number of those who were loyal to him, went to (the then-small) Prospect Mortgage. Together they helped grow the company using all of the activities, tools, and processes he'd formulated, refined, and perfected over the years. Many have remained since his retirement in 2016.

I once heard someone describe the new Ralph as Richard the Lion-hearted. It's appropriate. He used his warrior skills to coach himself and his team through the fear and turmoil that existed into a much better emotional and professional place. Not surprisingly, he succeeded, and so did they.

TOM NINNESS

EXPLODING YOUR SPHERE OF INFLUENCE: THE MOVIE STAR APPROACH

Told to and shared by Cindy

———————————⬧⬧⬧———————————

It usually takes me more than three weeks to prepare
a good impromptu speech.

—MARK TWAIN

TIMELINE	EMPLOYER	ROLE
During the 2007–2008 Financial Crisis	Cherry Creek Mortgage	Branch Manager
2017	New American Funding	Regional Manager

BEFORE TOM NINNESS had more than 9,000 closed transactions to his credit, he worked in retail sales at Venture department store. He was putting in twelve-, thirteen-, sometimes fourteen-hour days in the early 1980s, earning $1,400 a month. By the time Tom paid his rent of $460, his utilities, and put food on the table, there was not much left over. Moreover, with his long days, he had very little quality time at home. At twenty-six years old, Tom knew he needed a career instead of a job if he wanted to provide for his family in the way he and his wife, Pam, wanted for themselves and their newborn son.

The couple decided their first step was to open the door to opportunity so it could come knocking. While Tom continued to go to work every day at Venture, Pam sent resumes out on his behalf for positions in a wide variety of professions. The only prerequisite the couple had was that the job did not involve retail sales. They did not let Tom's lack of experience in other fields stop them. The first non-retail responder to schedule a meeting was Mortgage Associates (later Fleet Mortgage). After several interviews with them, Tom entered into his new career as a loan officer.

The position was more than a chance to earn higher wages. It elevated Tom's stature to that of a professional, which also shifted how he saw himself. To understand what an accomplishment this was for him, we need to take a look at his background. Tom came from a rough upbringing. Alcoholism and dysfunction were the only models he had known in his household. He was a very angry young man, which led him into trouble through his junior and high school years. His last appearance in front of the judge was a wake-up call. He could continue turning into his father or he could choose to have a different life. He chose the latter. Tom made the decision to go to college. To make this happen he worked two jobs while attending school full-time. Tom was the first to graduate college in his family. Even better, he met Pam in his second year at Central Michigan University where he earned his bachelor's degree in business education.

Tom had never been involved with real estate lending in his life. He had never even owned a home, nor was he sure, when or if that was going to happen. But that did not stop him. To illustrate how *really* green he was, Tom told me that during his first week at Mortgage Associates, he spelled the word "mortgage" as "morgage" on a critical document, because he hadn't heard the letter "t" pronounced. He laughingly said he could attribute his error to his Detroit education.

DISCIPLINE + DETERMINATION = SUCCESS

Unlike the emerging trend of paying loan officers basis points, Tom's starting salary at Mortgage Associates was $1,100 per month with a tiered commission scale. The base pay was a reduction from his previous job, but Tom and Pam both agreed, it was worth it to get out of retail, and explore a new line of work. The company paid a flat fee per file as an added incentive at certain milestones. The scale started over each month. Here's how it was tiered:

Closed Units per Month:

- First ten: $10 per loan closing.

- Next five: $25 per loan closing.

- Next five: $50 per loan closing.

- Twenty plus: $100 per loan closing.

Tom knew he was going to have to dedicate himself to some long hours, but he had done that before. The difference was that now he had the potential to earn the kind of paycheck he desired. Tom definitely had the drive to reach the auspicious goal of closing twenty-plus loans a month. This meant tapping into his endurance trait, which involved exerting the effort and persistence needed to accomplish his goals. Tom was unrelenting in his work habits and didn't give up easily on problems or challenges as they arose. Og Mandino once said, "Failure will never overtake me if my determination to succeed is strong enough." I believe this quote epitomizes the attitude Tom took, and it is still an integral component of his work ethic today.

Tom was taught that the best way to find leads for originating loans was to "pound the pavement." That meant taking the daily rate sheet to the local real estate offices, shooting the breeze, and asking for a deal. He performed this function every day without fail. The agents Tom visited continuously told him they did not have anyone who needed financing, and they probably would not any time soon. Rates were at their historical high point of 21 percent, resulting in homes selling sparingly, with many requiring creative financing to close.

An example of an unconventional resource that was often suggested and encouraged as a viable avenue by real estate agents was the wraparound mortgage, or land contract. The reason that this particular form of creative financing was so popular in the early '80s was because it gave buyers a better note rate than what they could get if they obtained a new loan by keeping the existing lender in the dark.

This arrangement consisted of an installment note between the seller and the buyer. The note encompassed the difference between the asking, or sales price, and the amount owed after the buyer's down payment. Based on a 10 percent down payment, with a sales price of $200,000, the deal was structured as follows:

SELLER SIDE (VENDOR):		BUYER SIDE (VENDEE):	
Purchase Price:	$200,000.00	First Mortgage:	$150,000.00
10% Down:	($20,000.00)	Difference:	$30,000.00
Remaining:	$180,000.00	Seller Note:	$180,000.00

The buyer benefited by receiving the seller's lower interest rate on the underlying instrument. However, it also left them in a precarious position, because the legal title remained in the seller's name until the existing lien had a zero balance. If for any reason the seller did not use the funds as intended and pay the mortgage when it was due, the lender would have the right to foreclose. There were instances when the existing lender did become aware of the change in ownership, even if the payment was paid on time. Both situations put the new homeowner in jeopardy of losing their entire investment, causing a legal quagmire. It wasn't until the unencumbered property was conveyed into their name via a recorded deed that the buyer had legal title.

Talk about an environment that was tough to work in. For the most part, all Tom could do was ask the agents he called on to think of him as soon as they had an opportunity available. Even though he consistently heard "No," Tom kept plugging away. Were there times he was discouraged? Of course, there were, but that didn't stop him. He is a testament to what dedication and persistence can achieve.

Tom is a friendly, extremely down-to-earth person, but even with his winsome and charismatic personality, it *still* took him six months before he originated his first loan. The referral was a refinance from one of the agents he had been diligently calling on. The borrower's loan had a 16.5 percent interest rate. By the time he concluded his second year, mortgage rates had steadily begun to decline, landing within the 13 percent range. Tom's dedication paid off. That year, he was the second-highest producing loan officer in his organization.

Fleet's management paid close attention to Tom's rapid success. When a set of circumstances occurred in the Phoenix, Arizona, office that required abrupt action, the Senior Vice President of sales thought immediately of him. After discovering fraudulent activities, removal of the existing branch manager and members of the sales team was mandated. The VP wanted to promote Tom to that position. After discussing the relocation with Pam, he accepted the position.

Management terminated the existing branch manager the same day Tom arrived at the Phoenix office, in October 1983. The remaining three employees immediately quit upon hearing the news. It was during those first few weeks, Tom said, that he learned the allure of drinking coffee extensively. There was many a night Tom burned the midnight oil typing final loan documents on an electric typewriter literally one keystroke at a time for clients who were left behind by the previous team.

While Tom was putting all his effort into bringing his new branch back to life, Pam and the kids tried to adjust to the Arizona lifestyle, but it just wasn't a good fit for them. They wanted to get back to a four-season climate. Tom's number one priority was to provide for his family and that meant paying attention to their needs. Though moving would mean a starting over, Tom went to his supervisor and said he would need to tender his resignation if a transfer was not available. A little more than a year had passed before Tom made his request. Fleet agreed and offered to transfer him to Denver—an office they were planning to close due to lack of production. Tom and Fleet agreed to a one year time frame to turn the office around; if it didn't work, then all parties would shake hands and part ways.

BUILDING A BLOCKBUSTER PERSONA

The move meant Tom would have to build his customer base from the ground up. He was okay with this. As with his transition from retail sales to mortgage lending, Tom didn't let the unknown stop him. To get a jump on things, he knew he needed to generate major momentum. Tom decided to adapt the same promotional concepts applied to blockbuster movies, by making his arrival an event worth noticing. Tom's first step was to design a flyer to mail to all the local real estate, title and closing agents a month before he was due to start. The message was simple and direct:

Top Producer

Tom Ninness

To Arrive in Denver Soon

His assistant followed up on the announcement by reaching out to all the individuals that were sent his flyer. The purpose of the call was to let them know how important it was to him to meet with that particular individual on a one-on-one basis. The tone Tom wanted to convey was similar to that of having your favorite A-list movie star wanting to get to know you. His end goal was to preschedule as many appointments as possible before his arrival at the new location.

By having someone else manage the arrangements, Tom was tapping into another fundamental that I call the third-party endorsement. This principle demonstrates one's level of success without being boastful. The scripting that Tom provided to his associate sounded something like this: "We're excited to inform you that our highest producer, Tom Ninness, is relocating from Phoenix to Denver. He has heard wonderful things about you. Tom *really* wants to get to know you. Is there a time that works best for the two of you to meet?"

Once a meeting was solidified, his assistant offered to be available on Tom's behalf until he arrived in Denver. The execution of his plan created the stir he was looking for. In fact, he had forty-five appointments lined up by the time he arrived in Colorado. Equally important to Tom were the meetings he had with the highly regarded title representatives in the area. His focus during those appointments was to learn everything he could about the individual and to garner their opinions on who he should get to know in the real estate community. Tom made sure to explain that while the number of transactions played a role in who he wanted to work with, he placed an even greater weight on other things, namely character, moral fiber, and ethics.

These get-togethers provided him with the inside track on both the heavy hitters *and* the up-and-coming agents to watch. By asking these account executives for their feedback, Tom captured their buy-in. The conversations naturally transitioned into Tom requesting their recommendation, which they often granted. Once again, the third-party endorsement strategy went into play. The best part about this brilliantly thought out two-step plan was the simplicity required to implement it. The cost factor was minimal, the results remarkable.

The other contributing factor to Tom's early success in Denver was his initial membership with the Aurora Association of REALTORS®. Tom joined the board with member status, which was quite ingenious, because loan officers typically joined as affiliates. The initial investment of $50 entitled him to receive a list of all the active broker/owner associates. By tactically spending time with the right people, Tom was able to grow his business swiftly and exponentially. That was just one more tool in his arsenal. Almost twenty-five years ago, he moved his membership over to the South Metro Denver REALTORS® Association.

THE MORE YOU KNOW

After reading *Love is the Killer App* by Tim Sanders, Tom shifted the format in which he performed his house calls with his professional partners. The author discusses the three-legged milk stool principle. These fundamentals center on sharing knowledge freely within an individual's network, without any strings attached. From that point on, Tom shifted his focus from concentrating all of his efforts on one person at a time, to capturing the attention

of *everyone* in the office by putting together fifteen- to thirty-minute educational presentations. Tom's content varied. Sometimes he discussed the
impact of new regulations, and ways to increase opportunity via new loan
programs. Other times he addressed effective lead generation campaigns,
sales techniques, economic and market conditions, and many other pertinent topics. This change in business model escalated Tom's role from loan
officer to educator, just as it had for Mike Smalley.

Tom went on to expand his audience to include the novice investor who
wanted to gain wealth though the acquisition of real estate. Finding attendees to fill the seats for this monthly event was not difficult. He had been
keeping track of the borrower's long-term financial goals for fifteen years or
more on a supplemental page to the loan application. A concept he learned
at Sales Mastery.

Table 1: Portion of Supplemental Page to Track Long-Term Financial Goals

How would you describe your financial philosophy?		
☐ Conservative	☐ Moderate risk taker	☐ Risk taker

Do you participate in a 401K or retirement plan at work? ☐ Yes ☐ No	If yes, how much do you have invested (total amount)?

Please mark the items below that are important to you in achieving your mortgage goals? (Check all that apply)

☐ Lowest payment	☐ Eliminate other debt	☐ Lowest down payment
☐ Lowest closing costs	☐ Maximum tax benefit	☐ Other _____
☐ Improve credit history	☐ Paying the loan off or down quickly	_____

Please mark the items below that are important to you in achieving your financial goals? (Check all that apply)

☐ Education on buying investment property	☐ Moving into a larger home in ___ years
☐ Building your net worth	☐ Buying investment properties
☐ Achieving financial freedom	☐ Debt reduction techniques
☐ Funding a mortgage retirement account	☐ Funding college education(s)
If so, when do you plan to retire? ___ Yrs	☐ Other _____

This model is premised on collecting extra information at the time of the initial interview. Depending on your customer base, these questions may vary. To gain greater insight and to be of service to the clientele, Tom feels it's critical to have a thorough understanding of the borrower's:

- Financial Philosophy

- Retirement Planning

- Long- and short-term Financial Goals

- Risk Tolerance

A member of his team enters the data collected on the form into his CRM. This additional information helps Tom apply the teachings he learned from reading several books about car salesman Joe Girard.

JOE GIRARD'S LAW OF 250

Mr. Girard, a high-school dropout, started working at the age of nine. His first job was as a shoeshine boy. At thirty-five, he began his illustrious sales career in the auto industry. Fired from his first job for being too aggressive, Joe chalked it up to jealousy from his co-workers. He had already sold more vehicles in his short time at the dealership by himself than the rest of the salespeople combined since the beginning of the year. He remained at his second and last job from 1963 to until he retired in 1978. During that time, he sold 13,001 cars. That's right *13,001* cars! The Guinness Book of World Records has recognized him as the world's greatest salesman.

Based on his own childhood and the fact that both men shared similar backgrounds, it comes as no surprise that Tom could *completely* relate to Joe's story. He admired Joe's tenacity, but his real takeaway from what he read was Girard's Law of 250. The premise is that "Everyone knows 250 people in his or her life that they can influence with their opinions and experiences."

Just imagine if every borrower you worked with told everyone they knew (all 250 of them) how wonderful you are as a loan officer . . . or not. Joe's customer philosophy really struck a chord with Tom. It's what drove his need to enhance the customizations to his existing database so he could drill down even further on the information he was collecting. To meet his objectives, he sharpened the segmentation of his customers. Below is how he parses his base:

- A—Ambassadors

- B—Everyone else except "newbies"

- C—Newbies

Tom reserves one-on-one sessions for the contacts he categorizes as his "Ambassadors," or his "A's." This elite group of individuals influences a significant number of people. They have an essence match with Tom; meaning they are like-minded individuals. The "B" and "C" groups are invited to attend the various events he hosts. He also stays in touch by delivering content to them electronically. This is how Tom effectively allocates his time. Yet, with all that he has on his plate, he still maintains his daily discipline of reaching out to:

- Four closed clients

- Two potential referrals

- Four prospects

- Two active relationships

To illustrate the power of having a database, Tom spoke of a time he made the decision to purchase one from an originator that was leaving the area. He asked if she planned to remain in contact with her customers after she moved. The loan officer indicated that she wasn't sure if she was staying in the mortgage industry, so her plan was to shut it down. Even if she did originate from her new location she didn't feel she would be in the position to service her current clientele properly. Tom offered to purchase her database and asked the loan officer to come up with a price. The quote she gave him was $2,000. Tom felt that she had not placed enough value, and upped the ante to $15,000. This action really speaks to Tom's character. He could not in good conscious pay his colleague what he considered to be a devalued price. However, he did add a caveat to their agreement. In exchange for paying more, Tom asked her to write a letter of introduction with a sincere endorsement assuring the client that they were being left in equally capable hands.

Tom felt confident he had made a wise investment, and time proved him right. He was familiar with the individual's work habits and client mix. Tom knew he would be a good fit, based on his own standards and procedures. Sure, there were borrowers who went to another resource for their financing. However, within the first three months, Tom had recouped his initial investment back. He would continue to reap the rewards from his purchase for an additional eighteen months.

Tom was profiting in other ways too. Fourteen years ago, he rolled out one of his first programs, the Real Estate Investors Forum (REIF). Tom brought in guest speakers who had expertise in a variety of topics, including 1031 exchanges. The event attracted thirty families on average. Although some of the attendees were familiar with 1031 exchanges, not all understood the immense tax savings they provided. This section of the IRS code allows investors to defer capital gains on the sale of their current property as long as the funds in an "exchange" are for the acquisition of "like-kind" property that's used for business or investment purposes. The economic gain is deferred because the only thing that has changed is the asset with which the value is associated.

Another way that Tom effectively tapped into the information he had been collecting from his borrowers was to find out who was inside their inner professional circle. Clients who thought highly of any one of the professional partners listed in the table on the next page fell under Tom's radar as a person to consider as a subject matter expert for one of his programs.

Table 2: Borrower's Inner Professional Circle

Please include information on the following professionals you are associated with. We may require their assistance in obtaining additional information for your loan.			
	NAME AND COMPANY	E-MAIL ADDRESS	TELEPHONE NUMBER
Insurance Agent			
Accountant/CPA			
Financial Planner			
Legal Advisor			
Human Resources Director			

Tom still offers complimentary courses like REIF to his consumer base. The small group size creates an air of intimacy that has forged strong relationships among the participants, resulting in an amazing network of like-minded individuals. These sessions continue to expand steadily through word-of-mouth, as one out of seven attendee families share what Tom has to offer with others.

His audience has diversified, from mostly novices to a number of repeat attendees who are now professional investors. Tom attributes his reputation as an innovator to the teachings he learned from the book titled *Blue Ocean Strategy: How to Create Uncontested Market Space and Make Competition Irrelevant* by W. Chan Kim and Renee Mauborgne. The authors claim that the way to gain a foothold in a desired market is to search for space that's uncontested. They contend that those who step out into the "blue ocean" will be in a league of their own because they're not getting lost in the "red ocean" of competing in the same way.

While his competitors were busy treading water with their rate sheets and donuts, Tom was busy affecting the lives of many with sound, prudent financial plans. He didn't look at the real estate professional as the sole means to meet credit-worthy borrowers. Instead, he expanded his horizons to include CPAs and financial planners, a number of whom were a direct result of the names that came from his client's professional inner-circle. After getting to know them, he would extend an invitation to be a part of one of his panels. Tom only made the offer if he felt comfortable with their level of expertise and demeanor. By inviting their clients from each of their respective databases, Tom and all panelists benefited. Equally important, the up-and-coming financier was privy to exceptional material crafted by Tom and the presenters he had chosen—a win-win experience for all concerned.

Tom differentiated himself even further from the competition by co-founding the former www.openhouseweekend.org when it was legally acceptable. The website was designed for agents to post their open house listings. Because of the pressure-free shopping environment consumers often opted in for more information. This built a warm list for both the agents and loan officers Tom was supporting through his efforts. His desire to help others grow is that very thing that draws first-time buyers, experienced investors, and savvy professional partners to work with him. More notably, it is what has kept them loyal for more than thirty-eight years.

Fleet eventually wanted Tom to relocate to Anchorage, Alaska. As far as he was concerned, this was not an option. His family was happy; he didn't want, nor did he intend to uproot them. Instead, Tom accepted a position with Maryland National Mortgage Company as their regional Vice President. He remained with them for seven years until Nations Bank acquired Maryland National in July 1992. Nations had been forth coming with their intention to close Tom's branch. He started looking for a new home to hang his professional hat.

He accepted a position with Market Street Mortgage in Greenwood Village, Colorado. He spent the next two years opening up their new office and running operations. His next home was Cherry Creek Mortgage, where he worked for the next eighteen years, until June 2013. During that time Tom's responsibilities included overseeing three states, aiding with recruitment, and providing mentorship.

A DYNAMIC SALES MODEL LEGACY

Through all the external commotion of the Great Recession, Tom never strayed from his business model. As a result, his $50 million in production stayed stable. He didn't incur the potential negative impact that happened to others. Tom believes staying true to his convictions and methodologies is what kept him insulated during those tough years.

As we know, the years of the financial crisis were a very dark time for the mortgage industry as a whole. Companies were closing left and right. Originators exited as quickly as they entered. They had started in the business when underwriting guidelines were lax. As a result, there had not been a prior need to learn the fundamentals. However, with the change in tide, the lack of knowledge didn't cut it. Only those with the desire and the willingness to improve would remain standing. This is what led Tom to write his book *The 90 Day Journey to Your Sales Success*. He took what he has learned throughout his career to develop the material for his training course, sharing his knowledge with salespeople across the country. And just as the title indicates there are ninety straight days of action steps and tasks that have time-honored proven results.

More than 6,000 people have learned how to create a dynamic sales model built on the loyalty of borrowers and professional referral partners. Tom teaches this message on a local level once a month with attendance ranging from 50–150 per session. His largest event drew close to 250 attendees.

Tom's material is especially useful to individuals who are new to the industry, a group he loves to mentor. During his weekly Friday morning sessions, Tom strips out components from his book to share with the "newbies." When they meet, the focus is primarily on these elements:

- Lead generation

- Client loyalty

- Professional referral sources

This networking meeting and the other public speaking events Tom hosts have been *so* well received that they've expanded to a national level.

He continues to challenge his audiences to consistently go beyond their limits, by teaching the merits of intentional thinking, empowering people to be more aware of getting what they want, and making more astute decisions. Ralph Massella subscribes to the same ideology.

There's no question that these presentations have been an enormous contributor to Tom's success. It is important to recognize however, that it is the active maintenance of his database, which he created early on, that has allowed him to seize and capitalize on his opportunities. His follow-through ensures that none of his efforts are in vain.

Tom is in a different stage of his mortgage career now. He focuses his energy on making a difference in the lives of mortgage originators and branch managers with New America Funding, where he accepted a position in March 2015 after leaving Cherry Creek. Tom has tripled the company's volume in the Colorado region. His role there aligns with his desire to coach and mentor. While he still originates on a smaller scale to keep a pulse on the industry, he has begun transitioning his book of business to his son, Aaron. Applying the same principles as his dad, Aaron has been able to average $4 to $5 million a month in closings after eighteen months. His volume continues to grow with his father's tutelage. Tom Ninness's legacy lives on.

M A R K   R A S K I N

KNOW THE CLEANING LADY: BUILD A STRONG FAMILY CULTURE

Told to and shared by Cindy and Kathleen

———————◆※◆———————

During my second month of college, our professor gave us a pop quiz. I was a conscientious student and had breezed through the questions, until I read the last one: "What is the first name of the woman who cleans the school?

Surely, this was some kind of joke. I had seen the cleaning woman several times. She was tall, dark-haired, and in her 50s, but how would I know her name? I handed in my paper, leaving the last question blank. Just before class ended, one student asked if the last question would count toward our quiz grade.

"Absolutely," said the professor. "In your careers, you will meet many people. All are significant. They deserve your attention and care, even if all you do is smile and say hello." I've never forgotten that lesson. I also learned her name was Dorothy.

—AUTHOR UNKNOWN

TIMELINE	EMPLOYER	ROLE
During the 2007–2008 Financial Crisis	CTX Mortgage Company	Branch Manager
2017	PrimeLending	Branch Manager

THE PROFESSOR'S COMMENT in this quote really epitomizes the Mark Raskin that we have come to know and love. He's an authentic, humble person who cares about all people. Not just those who have power, money, notoriety, or influence. Regardless of an individual's role at a company or their stature within the community, Mark recognizes the value every person brings to the table. He treats them with respect and dignity, from the cleaning staff all the way up the ranks to the CEO. The way Mark sees it, you either like a person or you don't. You're either loyal or you're not.

So where did Mark's values stem from? He credits his dad, Mort, for teaching him how to treat others. His father came from a family of farmers who were hard-working people living in the tightly knit community of Sioux City, Iowa. A place where close relationships with family, friends, and the community are an integral part of growing up. Where Mark was raised, children went to school together, played sports, and did their part on the farm.

After college, Mort's uncle offered him a summer job at his car dealership in Dallas, Texas, which became his lifelong career. Eventually, with his uncle's blessing, he opened his own automobile dealership in 1950. Mort was one of the first dealers in Texas to move into the wholesale arena. Later, he would expand into additional states. During his entire fifty-three years in business, his dad always took the time to ask everyone he met up with, "How's your day going? How was your weekend?" He'd built a reputation for mentoring countless numbers of people helping them achieve personal success. Mark has definitely followed his father's example.

Although Mark observed for himself his dad's genuine interest in and caring for others, it wasn't as if Mort sat him down and said, "Son, treating people well is how you succeed in business." A sale wasn't the catalyst for how Mort dealt with a person, but rather the sale was the by-product of his actions. Mark feels blessed to have grown up with and learned from such a good man.

CONCEPTS IN ACTION

Just as his dad was before him, Mark is a colleague, friend, and mentor. Throughout our years in this business, Kathleen and I have attended many high-profile events, met with even higher profile people. The one commonality we've noticed among some is their lack of genuineness. Treatment often centers on whom you know *and* what that person can do for you. If an individual falls out of favor, they are no longer worth noticing. So why bring this up? To drive home the point home this is *not* who Mark Raskin is or what he is about.

Mark worked at the family car dealership while he earned his bachelor's degree in finance at the University of Tulsa and his master's degree in administrative science from the University of Texas at Dallas. And, though Mark has deep admiration for his dad, working in the family business wasn't his life's goal. His job paid the bills, but the habitual routine of what he did, day in and day out, was not gratifying. Mark didn't feel disgruntled or frustrated at his job, but he did realize that that working at the dealership wasn't his passion.

While attending a funeral in late 2001, Mark ran into a friend of his who worked at CTX Mortgage Company. After catching up a bit, the two of them agreed to a time to meet for lunch. While they were eating their meal, Mark's dissatisfaction with his profession came up in the conversation. His friend suggested to Mark that he consider coming to work with him, and then began to explain why he thought mortgage lending would be a good option for him. As the lunch hour progressed, Mark had an "aha" moment. Although writing mortgages were foreign to him, finance wasn't nor was working within a corporate structure. It was, in fact, a framework he knew well and had thrived under.

Just as he does today, before engaging in a new relationship Mark asked himself, *Why would I want to do business with this person?* In this case, his friend was extremely honest, his customer care was off the charts, and he had an amazing work ethic. He went to every loan closing, even if there was an hour commute involved. Mark knew this for a fact because of the treatment his referrals received when he sent them to him. Mark admired his friend because he always took care of business; even in difficult circumstances, he didn't try to BS his way out of it. He never played the avoidance or blame game. That was why Mark was willing to do business with him. The value he puts on these factors is demonstrated throughout this chapter.

Mark knew why he felt comfortable being associated with his friend, but he needed to take these questions one step further. With the first part of the equation in check, it was time to get the answer to the second part, *Why would I want to do business with this company?* He needed to be sure that the organization's culture was the right fit for him. Earnings was a factor, but it wasn't a deciding one. Mark wasn't interested in companies that conducted business with a hope and a prayer. He's not a wing-it kind of person.

Mark appreciated CTX's comprehensive training program. The company offered a clearly defined approach to sales with a proven record of accomplishment. They also had a reputation of attracting and keeping high-producing originators. Mark realized why when he joined them in January 2003. The company had a family culture. Everyone was important as an individual; they weren't just a number. Each employee had a clear understanding of what was expected of him or her. Because they felt appreciated, the staff strived to exceed CTX's standards time and time again.

One of the things Mark noticed at the onset of his mortgage career was that people like to work with positive and successful people. They're not drawn to failures or negativity. He credits his branch manager for learning this powerful lesson. After Mark was given the added responsibility of growing his branch, he went to his mentor and friend, Cathy Stroud, for her counsel. She was the central area regional manager for CTX. He wanted to know her formula for growing such a successful region.

Cathy shared with him that she conducted a litmus test every time she considered hiring or conducting ongoing business with an individual. The test had one question, "Am I willing to have this person over for Sunday dinner in my home?" If she could answer "Yes," Cathy continued cultivating the relationship. If the answer was "No," she would let it come to a graceful close. Mark had no difficulty incorporating this philosophy. As a result, he's been very successful in his recruiting efforts.

Mark didn't limit his power of observation to others. He also regularly evaluated his own performance. One of the things he noticed about himself was a lack of enthusiasm at intermittent times of the day. This was really apparent when he sat at his desk to make calls; his tone just didn't come across energetically. Mark came to the realization that he was slouching which contributed to his sluggishness. He fixed that by investing in a standup desk, which gave him the mobility he needed to exude and convey the energy he felt. Mark said it was amazing what a big difference this simple and cost-effective change made.

CUSTOMER CARE

The first time Cindy met Mark was in the early 2000s, when his branch manager hired her company, CD Consulting Group, to review the group's use of their Act!™ program. The two features the team made the most use of were the histories tab where they kept detailed records of previous conversations, and the proactive scheduling of communication, which could be viewed in the activities or calendar section of the program.

The first feature enabled the team to reconnect with the customer. Cindy witnessed firsthand how this worked when she shadowed Mark at his desk. She asked him for his rationale behind this step. Mark replied, "Performing this action allows me to re-familiarize myself on where the client and I last left off," he said. "Let's face it, we're all busy. The reality is that no matter how much any one of us would like to remember every single detail of the people we touch, it's virtually impossible. I believe taking the time to complete this added step before picking up the phone helps make the person I am talking to feel special. The customer feels like there is no one more important than they are, and in that moment there isn't. This is the glue that holds the relationship together when the competition comes courting."

The second feature prevented dormancy and neglect. If a forward activity isn't scheduled, then the originator can unintentionally forget the client, opening the door for the competition to step in. The reason Mark has no problem implementing his database system—where so many do—is because he consistently supersedes the expected experience he has promised to deliver. If a loan officer has over promised and under performed on their commitments, it's very difficult to ask for more business and referrals. This is often where the reluctance stems from. More than that, Mark really wants to know how little Timmy did at his Little League game, or how the piano recital turned out for Susie. His authenticity and consistency has earned him a successful career and has cemented the loyalty, respect, and admiration of his clients, professional partners, and team. To provide sound advice, Mark and his loan officers have always gone beyond asking the routine questions. They dig deeper in order to have a clearer understanding of what is currently happening in the customer's life. This enables them to be a more effective resource during the first and subsequent transactions. To gain clarification, here are some of the questions Mark and his team will ask at the time of the initial application:

- How long does the borrower plan to keep their mortgage?

- Are there any major changes happening in their life that they need to plan for? Such as:

  - The financing of college tuition(s).
  - A change in job position, earnings, or both.
  - A possible relocation in the near future.

- What does retirement look like and how does the customer plan to get there?

- Is the client presently employing a financial planner, and if so, are they satisfied with them? (If the borrower indicates their lack of satisfaction, Mark asks if they'd like him to provide recommendations.)

Knowing this information rather than assuming helps them to offer the best guidance possible to their clientele. Mark remains convinced that finding out his customers' short- and long-range goals is essential before voicing his recommendations. Advice that is always driven by what he feels is in the best interest of the client.

It's worth pausing to recognize Mark's evolution during his mortgage career. He has the ability to integrate sound fundamentals and make them his own. What he didn't do was mimic exactly what he observed. Instead, he took the parts that suited him and discarded the rest, a process that has enabled him to create a formidable recipe for successful execution.

WHY DO BUSINESS . . .

For the majority of his nearly seven years with CTX, Mark and the rest of the group enjoyed prosperous times. However, the collapse of the financial markets starting in 2007 began to take its toll, *even* on Centex, the parent company that employed them. Hundreds of retail lenders had closed their doors either by choice or were forcibly shut down by the regulators.

On behalf of himself and his team, Mark began the interviewing process in earnest in the fall of 2008. He followed the same format he used when he'd entered into lending by asking himself, *Why would I want to do business with this person/company?*

- How transparent is the culture?

- What is the company's reputation?

- What do their competitors say about them?

- Do they have employee longevity, or do they have constant turnover?

- Do they have genuine empathy for their staff, or is it all about the numbers?

- Who are the significant producers and what does their business model look like? Is it in alignment with the way our team does business?

- What are the steps operations takes to support production and vice versa?

Mark narrowed the playing field down to four contenders. In the end, he placed the most weight on the company that was smallest. His group had been through a very tumultuous time during the past eight months, and Mark's goal was to move to an opposite environment. He still sought a company that had systems in place and a corporate structure, but equally important, Mark wanted a home where his staff felt valued and cared for. He admits he had a misconception that the larger firms would have a harder time providing this atmosphere. He formed this opinion based on his own presumptions rather than from anything anyone said to him.

The majority of the CTX retail employees from the Texas location joined Mark at the new organization. They trusted his recommendation and were fiercely loyal to one another. Within a few days, however, Mark realized he'd made an error in judgment. He felt the company had overpromised and exaggerated their strengths. Immediately, Mark shared his concern with his staff and co-workers.

He was in a difficult situation. Mark had contractual obligations with the new firm. His intentions were not to hurt them, but he felt compelled to protect his team and business associates. Fortunately, his professional partners had such a high level of faith in his ability that the majority continued to refer their transactions to him. This was their way of standing behind him, even through all the turmoil.

Within six weeks of Mark's hire date, management decided to fire him. Before he even had the chance to share the news with his wife, Lisa, his phone began ringing off the hook with job offers. Mark said, it was the first full night's sleep he got since joining the company. As far as he was concerned, the firing was God's will.

In November 2008, after going through the interview process again, Mark made the decision to join PrimeLending. His personal team members and an underwriter joined him right away. During the next few months, the majority of those who'd followed him from CTX migrated over. To this day, Mark's personal team is still together. PrimeLending retains a significant number of the folks who joined the company in the latter part of 2008 and early 2009.

That's quite a testament to the loyalty Mark inspires. When asked what he attributes this to, Mark said he thinks of each team member as a partner, regardless of his or her job title. No one's above or beneath anyone else. In those instances where challenges arise and the transaction doesn't run smoothly, the team discusses what they need to change to prevent the situation from recurring. They don't play the blame game. Period. All these years later, Mark is still adopting what he learned from the observation of individual who introduced him into the mortgage industry.

Mark shared that there have been some hiring mistakes along the way. Individuals who didn't fit in. He's learned the best way to prevent this from happening is to hire slowly. He recommends taking the time to ask the right questions, such as the ones below, when conducting an interview.

- Name a difficult situation you've been in and what did you did to arrive at a resolution.

- In what areas are you looking to grow?

- How do you see yourself contributing to the growth of the team/branch/company?

- How can our organization contribute to your success?

- How would you describe your previous employment experiences? What did you learn? Looking back, do you feel these experiences gave you the opportunity to grow? How?

- What's your plan for generating lifelong clients?

When growing his branch, Mark noticed some applicants frequently flip-flopped between companies. He found that in many cases excessive movement is an indicator that, even though a candidate appears strong on paper, they still may not be a good fit. In his opinion, loyalty (both ways) is paramount! While it's necessary to complete background checks and due diligence, these steps are not the only barometer to use when considering people for employment. Another sign of a potential challenge down the line is individuals who only want to talk about signing bonuses. He believes anyone worth their salt will be more concerned with negotiating a higher commission split over a period of time rather than a one-time incentive.

Based on experience, Mark recommends all new loan officers train for a minimum of twelve to eighteen months as an assistant to learn the basics. However, his preference is to keep the mentorship relationship intact for several years. This enables the novice to learn more than the rudimentary basics of different loan programs. With the right tutelage, they also gain finesse in relationship management, insight on how to develop purposeful marketing, as well as learning the fundamentals on how to run their business as a business.

Not all employers offer this type of program. If that is your current situation, Mark recommends paying particular attention to what top producers are incorporating that works for you. Adapt and tweak as necessary to build processes that align with your way of doing business. This is exactly how Mark started his journey.

Mark believes that possessing knowledge is critical to establishing and maintaining trust. To sharpen his tools, he's attended several acclaimed sales trainings during his career. The XINNIX Mortgage Academy stressed the importance of methodically handling all aspects of sales. Mark feels that one of the most important concepts that XINNIX teaches is that there will always be things we don't like to do, but nonetheless, they still need doing. This is the same philosophy he learned from the friend who indoctrinated him into mortgage lending. Mark has also attended Todd Duncan's High Trust Sales Academy," where he learned the importance of finding out what referral sources partners, colleagues, and customers find valuable before offering his wares. It's not about you, it's about them and what they want. Our friend Jeff Lake adheres to this same philosophy.

One of the practices Mark and the team adopted early on and continue to keep as a cornerstone of their business model is attending every closing—again, a discipline he learned from his friend who got him started in mortgage banking. To manage their time effectively, Mark and other members of the sales team use their commute time driving to and from closings to call their spheres of influence. After the initial hello, the conversations often start out with, "I'm on my way to Fort Worth to attend a closing. I've been thinking about you and thought I'd give you a call to see how you're doing." The power in this language is huge.

Mark and his team are accomplishing two objectives. First, they're removing the sterilization often associated with making sales calls on a predetermined date and time. Second, and equally important, it maximizes how they spend their time during working hours. For Mark, this enables him to conclude his day sooner, providing more quality time at home with Lisa and their two children.

In 2009, Kathleen flew to Dallas to interview with some people from his company. Mark joined the executives and department heads that she had her meeting with. She was astounded that he chose to spend well over an hour with her, someone whom he had never met. Kathleen was further amazed after sending a note of thanks to the people she met with that Mark was the first to respond.

During Kathleen's years at PrimeLending, she watched his work style. He consistently met with recruits and followed up with all of them afterward. Mark produced and closed loan volume at the top of the list every year while volunteering for countless committees both within the company and in the mortgage industry.

Kathleen vividly remembers a time when Mark went above and beyond. In 2012, the executive team wanted to incorporate a panel discussion as part of the agenda at the upcoming annual sales rally. They thought it would be beneficial for the audience to hear firsthand what some of Prime's top referral sources wanted, needed, and liked. Mark recommended his superstar real estate agent, Seychelle Van Poole Engelhard, with Keller Williams to be one of the participants.

Mark orchestrated this concept brilliantly with the help of his agent and his colleague Chris Nooney. The three of them performed a spoof to highlight the differences between an exceptional loan officer and one who falls short. At the start of the skit, Mark and Seychelle are in the process of conducting their discovery session. They are interrupted with the constant ringing of her cell phone. When she finally answers, the audience becomes privy to a conversation between Seychelle and a fictitious loan officer, portrayed by Chris. The conversation demonstrates what not to do when attempting to build rapport. Once the call ends, Seychelle shared her expectations and definition of a business partner:

1. Both parties will truly need to be the best at what they do; this is a bare minimum to get in the door.

2. Both need to have each other's backs before, during, and after the transaction so the customer has a seamless experience.

3. Mutually, they're looking for opportunities to grow together.

4. The loan officer attends all closings since the buyer's questions are always about the loan.

5. The originator is willing to refer business back to her, and if they cannot do that, they will put in some sweat equity.

When asked to define what she meant by the term "sweat equity," Seychelle replied, "Hosting open houses together, knocking on doors together, hosting first-time buyer and investor seminars, anything we can do together to grow business. This could also mean recommending each other on LinkedIn. I think the most important thing is cross-promoting each other during the transaction so the buyer feels as though they have a real team working on their behalf. That way, our borrowers are more likely to refer their friends to both of us."

To further the session's lightness, Mark used a technique he had just encountered while attending a Broadway musical in New York City, where, throughout the production, the audience heard the voice of God. In Mark's production, he had an announcer who spoke from offstage. Once the interactions between the parties hit a natural break, the voiceover would drive the salient points home. Their skit was the hit of the rally by far. It's worth watching on YouTube.[1]

UNPARALLELED DEDICATION

Mark's team shares his values, sales approach, and commitment to clients. This is articulated on his LinkedIn profile: "Our business is built largely on referrals. We pride ourselves on growing through outstanding mortgage lending experiences so that all parties involved are proud to refer their friends, family, and acquaintances for our services . . . It is our utmost priority to bring integrity and competitive value to our clients, our team members, our partners, and our company." This statement is not written lightly or as a matter of public relations. The team has taken the time to clearly recognize, define, and articulate their core convictions, which they use internally.

CORE CONVICTIONS OF THE RASKIN TEAM

+ Integrity

    - We always do the right thing, period.
    - We are honest in everything we do.
    - We do what we say and never offer what we cannot deliver.

+ Leadership

    - We provide true value both internally and externally.
    - We believe in education for not only our team members, but our clients as well. Our clients will have an educated confidence in their decisions.

+ Serve

    - We help our clients and team members achieve their dreams to the best of our ability.
    - We care about and respect our clients and team members.
    - We always place our client's needs in front of our own.

+ Loyalty

    - We approach all decisions with a mutual concern and loyalty to our clients, partners, and team members.
    - Our primary focus is on relationships first, and the underlying transactions second.

+ Excitement

    - We encourage excitement within our team, clients and partners, through our experiences in working together.

RESULTS ARE OVERWHELMING

The tenets of the Raskin Team's core convictions are not fluff, but a way of life supported by action, as illustrated by a couple of comments we found on the Yelp™ website. Originally founded in 2004 to "help people find great local businesses like dentists, hair stylists, and mechanics," Yelp has not typically been associated with finding a credible mortgage professional. Yet at the time of this publication, we found over fifty comments from individuals raving about their experience with Mark and his team. These two unsolicited testimonials are just a small sample:

> "Mark is more than a guy who can get you a home loan for a purchase or refi, he becomes a trusted advisor. He's not going to steer you one way to make an extra buck, he's looking to make your life better by getting you in the right mortgage for where you are right now. He's looking ahead to other goals you might have, and taking that all into consideration."

> "I was a first-time homebuyer for a modest house in Missouri and Mark gave me only first-class service. [Mark was] always available for consultation and always patient to explain the home-buying process. Mark believes in developing relationships, not pushing sales. I will definitely use him again and would recommend him to anyone wanting a reliable and knowledgeable loan officer."

Mark's clients are not the only ones who've noticed his unparalleled dedication. For several years, *D Magazine*™ has named Mark on its list of Best Mortgage Professionals. He has earned the prestigious Chairman's Circle designation as a PrimeLending Power Producer every year since 2009. During his time at CTX, he earned the National Sales Leadership Award. This was how the company recognized individuals such as Mark for "exhibiting outstanding salesmanship, an affinity for teaching, company loyalty, a teamwork mentality; a commitment to excellence, a sense of humor, and a dedication to serving others."

He has also developed a noteworthy reputation in national circles. Mark has represented Texas in the Future Mortgage Leader's program sponsored by the Mortgage Bankers Association through which scholarships are awarded to qualified recipients.

Mark is very involved with the Texas Mortgage Bankers Association. He has been on the board as a director since 2008. Mark became the Secretary/Treasurer in 2015/2016, the Vice President for 2016/2017, and currently serves as the President for the 2017/2018 term. Rarely is a commissioned person appointed to this executive role. He finds serving in this capacity is a great way to give back to an industry that has been, in his words, very kind to him.

Clearly, Mark has a lot on his plate. When asked how he accomplishes all that he does, and still have work and life balance, Mark said he attributes his success in this area to his current coach, Bill Hart at Building Champions. Bill has helped him stay on track with his priorities by creating and, more importantly, actually *living* his life plan. He keeps this document within arm's reach at all times. Mark continues to amass information and skills that assist him in becoming even more proficient at what he does. Because as a leader, you had better know what you are doing. Too many people are depending on you.

KAREN DEIS

SELL YOUR EXPERIENCE: ONE-STOP SHOPPING IN ELECTRIC STILETTOS

Told to and shared by Cindy

———————————⊱✖⊰———————————

> The odds of going to the store for a loaf of bread and coming out with
> only a loaf of bread are three billion to one.
>
> —ERMA BOMBECK

TIMELINE	EMPLOYER	ROLE
During the 2007–2008 Financial Crisis	LoanOfficerTraining.com	President/Founder
Present Employer 2017	LoanOfficerTraining.com	President/Founder

KAREN DEIS DIDN'T BEGIN her illustrious career in the mortgage business. In fact, if fate hadn't intervened, she might still be in a job that didn't motivate or stimulate her. She had been working as a purchasing agent for several years in the paint and siding industry. Karen had learned the functions of her job and performed them exceedingly well. Her core responsibilities consisted of ordering product and expediting the delivery of that product to ensure it was on time—processes that would serve her well in the profession she was about to enter. While she was gaining her experience, Karen was highly motivated; however, when it became clear that she'd reached the pinnacle for that position, she started to lose interest. Uninspired, Karen realized she needed to spread her wings if she was going to grow.

Fate interceded on her behalf. The employment agency she applied through sent her to Waterfield Mortgage for her first interview. The year was 1972, April Fool's Day to be exact. Karen landed the receptionist job. Three weeks after her start date, her boss offered her the closing agent position. Even though she had no idea what a closing was all about, or what a closing agent did, she figured she'd learn what she needed to along the way.

Staying true to her adventurous spirit, Karen made the move to sales within a few years. Sure, the idea of working on commission was scary, but that was also part of the thrill. She took a leap of faith in herself, becoming the first female loan officer in her hometown of South Bend, Indiana. By her third year, Karen ranked as one of the top producers in the company. She advanced to branch manager, and then progressed to Regional Vice President.

By the early '80s, Karen's sales and management career was moving along at a steady clip when her company wanted her to take on a big challenge. They asked Karen to turn around a regional office in Houston, Texas. It was going down the tubes due to mismanagement, high default, and practically no name recognition whatsoever. She agreed. When Karen arrived on the scene, her company was ranked 298 in the state for closed-loan volume. At first, that position might not sound too bad, but that was out of 302 companies. After four years under her guidance, the branch moved up to number eight. Karen gets it done, and gets it done well.

LIFE ALTERING EVENT #1

A major event that shaped Karen's mortgage career occurred while she was still working at the Houston branch. It turned out to be a professional life-changer. On the surface, the transfer of a loan to one's organization is a routine occurrence. This particular deal, however, had to close by Christmas

Eve, 1986. That gave Karen and her team only a two-week window when four was more the norm. Though the agent received warnings that the deadline was unrealistic, Karen's group promised to do their best to accommodate the request. The loan didn't fund as planned and, as a result, the real estate agent was not happy. After listening to a series of phone tirades, Karen knew something had to change, because she wasn't willing to be treated that way.

That night, Karen reached what some might call a tipping point. She made the decision to take control of her destiny. After all, why should she be held hostage by, and take verbal abuse from, someone selling two to three homes a year? There was, and still is, a plethora of buyers out in the universe. Why, indeed? This is when Karen began to formulate her consumer-direct strategy.

It's important to recognize that Karen didn't take the easy way out. She didn't sit and fume. She didn't complain about how unfair life is then do nothing about it. No. Instead, Karen took a course of action that would be a huge conceptual shift in how she acquired business. One week later, right after January 1, 1987, Karen commenced her new marketing campaign.

First things first, she had to generate potential leads that she could market to. Apartment complexes seemed like a good place to start. Simply because it was likely that the current tenants didn't own a home but would want to someday. Since the business of buying lists didn't exist at that time, she had to create her own. Karen hired a couple of reliable college kids who needed to make some extra spending money. They were thrilled with her rate of $10 per hour; minimum wage at that time was $3.35. The students were more than willing to follow the process she expected them to adhere to. The steps required were simple and absolute:

1. Physically walk around the apartment complex.

2. Write down the address and number of each unit.

3. Confirm the ZIP code associated with the complex.

4. Enter the information into a Microsoft® Excel® spreadsheet.

Karen's assistant sent postcards to the renters who were on her list. The cards promoted the free reports Karen had produced. Topics included how recipients could save money and make wise choices. Some of the more popular tag lines that produced results were:

- Are you tired of paying your property owner's mortgage?

- How to avoid the nine most costly mistakes when purchasing a home.

- Ask these seven questions before hiring a real estate professional.

Karen was very clear about her call to action; she didn't confuse the issue with a multitude of mixed messages. If an individual was interested in owning a home, they needed to call her office to receive their free report. The function of the mailers was to attract traffic, which they did beautifully. The creation of the list in combination with the mailers became phase one in the development of her lifecycle marketing plan.

Karen knew that when the calls started to roll in she'd need a way to keep track of each caller so she could follow-up with them on a consistent basis. There would be no point to going to all the effort of marketing to and talking with potential clients if it didn't reap the reward of closing their loans. Karen also wanted to know which mailers worked, and which ones did not the produce the results she was expecting.

It's critical to take a moment to understand the importance of this second phase. It's easy to get caught up in the initial momentum, but if you neglect to compound your efforts with an effective follow-up plan those efforts are wasted. This is why having a database system is so very important. After a thorough investigation of software products, Karen selected the Act!™ program. The price point and ease of use met her needs.

When a renter called in, they were invited to attend her one-hour workshop: Mistakes Homebuyers Make When Buying a Home. Regardless of whether a person chose to attend, Karen always requested permission to stay in touch. Once obtained, she added their complete contact information and any pertinent notes from their conversation into her database. A systematic follow-up campaign was assigned. This was how Karen nurtured her leads throughout the early days of their budding relationship.

On average, she invited 500 prospects from her growing list. Typically, from a list that size, 30 people would show-up on the appointed day and time. At the start of each workshop, Karen explained in her opening remarks that one of her gifts to the attendees was a free credit report. A practice, which was legally acceptable back then. If individuals were interested, they needed to sign the authorization form that was left on their chair prior to the commencement of the event. This gave the consent needed to run their credit. About 80 percent liked the idea and provided their signatures.

As Karen began her presentation, her assistant, Jenna collected the signed papers. While the session progressed, Jenna ran the credit checks, placing each report in a sealed envelope. Included was a cover letter stating that Karen would be calling within two days to review. Participants received the materials at the end of the evening. Typically, one or two families scheduled their consultation that same night. The balance still received a call from her no later than the promised two days. However, it was rare they had to wait that long. Karen's philosophy was to strike while the iron was hot. As a result, they often heard from her the next day. Before hanging up the phone, she fulfilled her next call to action, which was to schedule a face-to-face meeting to go over financing options.

Because the next step was such an integral part of her strategy to convert prospects to client status, Karen made sure that her calendar wasn't over-scheduled. She also called those who had sent in an RSVP but didn't show. All meeting attendees, along with anyone else they brought as a guest, were added to her monthly newsletter distribution. Karen didn't use a canned version, instead, she created her own publication that included:

- A spotlight on one or two customer stories.

- Short articles from affiliate partners.

- Something personal about Karen (such as a family event or celebration).

- Hot topics of the month.

She knew not everyone would read her newsletter. Karen didn't let that stress her out. No, what she cared about was being front and center. The circulars she sent out—the same ones she used for her apartment complex prospects—did exactly that for her. Every month, they went out like clockwork. It's important to note that sending out her publication didn't replace picking up the phone and reaching out to her customer base. Rather, it was another method of staying in touch. Karen made calls at pre-determined intervals based on the client's future lending needs and/or life changes that could have an impact on their finances. After all the time she had spent cultivating these individuals, Karen wasn't going to risk losing potential business to her competitors. She clearly understood the importance of being available at the right time.

Karen had come up with a unique strategy that separated her from the competition. Equally noteworthy, she understood the importance of tracking her results, which is how she knew which postcard made the phone ring. After a while, it became clear that the three taglines previously mentioned generated higher quality prospects. These individuals typically found value in going to Karen's workshop. They were highly motivated, often purchasing a home within a ninety-day window.

Three decades later, Karen can still recite her conversion numbers from her efforts: 10 percent would buy a home within sixty days; 20 percent would take action within six months; another 20 percent would buy within a year; and the remaining 50 percent were in situations that prevented them from buying. Leases, credit issues, job stability, and/or lack of savings were some of the reasons people couldn't move forward. And there were also those that just weren't interested in doing what it took to own a home.

During her career, Karen solicited roughly 2,500 individual apartment units. Similar to most direct mail campaigns, the return had a 1–2 percent response rate. When she reached full throttle, Karen received twenty to twenty-five phone calls per mailing. Eventually, she hired software developers to create a program to build her lists electronically. Later this idea morphed into one of the products she recently sold: Apartment Tool Kit. Loan officers who implement this strategy might consider sending their invitations electronically in addition to, or instead of, print mail, using an opt-in format for the RSVP.

LIFE ALTERING EVENT #2

Karen's next professional life-altering event occurred in the late '80s when her boss was fired for fraud. The new replacement, wanted her to act in a similar manner, expecting Karen to have the same moral compass as her former manager. She was unwilling to walk that tightrope. Karen felt that she had to report what was being asked of her to the president of the company. When she didn't receive the support she was expecting, Karen realized it was time to move on.

The decision to move back to Indiana from Houston was a very easy one for her. She and Becky, one of her eight siblings, had been discussing the idea of opening their own mortgage company for years. Why wait? Once Karen got settled in South Bend, she and Becky founded Cornerstone Mortgage. Karen had been contemplating the idea of a one-stop shop for a while. When she didn't see a downside she formed her own real estate and appraisal company in 1990. This enabled her to offer these services at a discounted rate, setting her apart from the competition. It was the first one of it's kind in the area, and possibly in the entire region.

They specialized in conventional "A" paper financing—vanilla thirty- and fifteen-year fixed rate mortgages—with new construction as their niche. Together they were able to solidify a controlled business arrangement (CBA) with Weiss Homes, one of the largest builders in northern Indiana. Karen and Becky capitalized on their apartment complex strategy by offering to share their list with the builder provided he take over the distribution of the postcards. It was a win-win situation increasing the profitability for Cornerstone while generating prospects for Weiss. Their business acumen and entrepreneurial spirit earned these two amazing women almost

60 percent of Weiss Home's new construction deals increasing their production by 40 percent.

After five-years of soliciting apartments, both in conjunction with builders and on their own, it was clear that the sales cycle they encountered was an extended one. This made for an outstanding long-term plan. But Karen felt the need to find a solution that would shorten the progression from lead to closed sale. So she formulated the idea to put together a comprehensive employee benefit package.

Cornerstone expanded upon their consumer-direct strategy by targeting organizations within a fifty-mile radius. As the ideas continued to germinate, Karen's attraction to corporate marketing heightened. She realized this untouched market segment gave her borrowers who were ready, willing, and able. They could perform in a shorter time frame than the apartment complexes she was marketing to. Many were relocating, looking to buy a home in the immediate future. Karen's approach was both simple and tactical. Instead of starting her list from scratch, her first step was to use the power of her database. She had been segmenting her customers for years. Her software allowed her to run a search by employer, providing a list of all employees who worked at the specific companies the sisters wanted to target. Karen put on her marketing hat and proceeded full steam ahead.

Step one was to reach out to the clients who worked for these organizations. A member of the team asked for a letter of recommendation, indicating their intent to forward it to the president of the company they worked for. Karen can't remember a single person turning down the request. Once they received three or four endorsements, they would include them with a letter of introduction and put them in the mail. The envelope was addressed to the president and marked confidential, ensuring it remained unopened and was delivered to the intended party.

The body of the introduction indicated Karen's office would be calling to schedule an appointment to discuss how Cornerstone's employee benefit package assisted with recruitment and retention. The format followed the same theme as the cover letter provided at her seminars. Karen would conduct the presentation, but an assistant booked the appointment. The rationale behind this step was to convey Karen and the president were on an equal playing field.

The purpose of the letters of recommendation was to establish Karen's credibility. Her ultimate goal was to sign-up at least one company a month. To accomplish this, the team needed to send out a minimum of five letters on a monthly basis. Karen's process was on target. Two to three appointments were generated from these mailings, which led to a commitment from at least one company who agreed to implement her program. That equates to a 90 percent success rate!

Congruently, Karen was busy negotiating with industry related partners to obtain a reduction in the cost of services they offered. Real estate agents, insurance providers, escrow, title, and moving companies participated. Her team also contacted local merchants who were requested to participate as well. On average, these vendors discounted their products and services 10–15 percent. Altogether, the savings amounted to nearly $1,000. This was a significant amount of money in 1992. Taking inflation into account the cost savings equates to roughly $1,730.

To make sure she didn't violate the Real Estate Settlement Procedures Act (RESPA) guidelines, Karen had her compliance department review her endeavor before launching. After feeling assured that the reduced fees were true discounts and not an inducement for business, Karen received the blessing she sought. Her program was RESPA compliant. She was ready to launch.

The plan Karen put together was a win-win for all concerned. From the employer's perspective, the bottom line improved due to increased retention. Instead of being nomadic, employees saw the value of putting down roots, reducing the inclination to be transient. They had a good job with steady income making homeownership more appealing. Additionally, companies were provided with a competitive edge when recruiting candidates. Karen and her team had brought in a new innovative twist that didn't cost the employer a cent. From Karen's perspective, she was leveraging her presence. Rather than limiting herself by touching only one person at a time, she kept in front of the masses with her paycheck stuffers and the workshops that she conducted during the allotted time for lunch or after hours.

Employees who were in the process of relocating benefited from the reduction of stress involved when moving to a new area. In advance, they were sent information about the surrounding area, including school districts, shopping, community organizations, and upcoming events. Real estate agents saw an increase in sales because of their participation in the program. The reduction of the agent's commission translated into lower purchase prices, an additional credit towards closing costs or both. Buyers were ecstatic to receive this additional perk. For those needing financing, Karen and her team were ready and able to provide a *stress-free, smooth* experience.

To get the word out, they placed posters and pamphlets in the break rooms. Information about becoming pre-approved as well as tips on buying, selling, or refinancing were literally at an employee's fingertips. The importance of hiring the right professionals was a consistent message—not doing so could mean incurring costly mistakes.

Although she didn't have a size requirement for the companies she approached, Karen found that the smaller firms of five hundred or fewer had a greater level of intimacy among the staff. Employees tended to discuss what was going on in their lives during their free time. Many were either already friends or became friends outside of work. What was significant about this dynamic was the frequency in which homeownership was the primary topic of conversation. This meant Karen's group was included in these discussions. Once her benefit program was fully entrenched into an organization's culture, the employees did the majority of the selling. This is a fantastic example of building an external sales force. The endorsements stemming from this program kept rolling in.

The advantage of working with firms larger than 500 in size was that they had a higher rate of relocation. The company either recruited into the area or they transferred employees to another location. Either way, opportunity abounded. The spectrum ranged from first-time and move-up buyers, to those who wanted to refinance their existing property for a variety of reasons. Reduction in payment, pulling cash-out for debt consolidation, home improvement, or acquiring another home, are prime examples.

One high-profile client in particular gave Karen's program real liftoff. He was the president of the local Teamsters Union. In the course of taking his loan application her client mentioned that he was up for reelection. Karen immediately piggybacked on that comment, recommending he consider offering what she had done for many of the local businesses. She provided him with the details of how her employee benefits program worked. Karen suggested that by offering to his membership, he would have a definite advantage over the other contenders by providing this novel and useful service. Her client was *so* impressed he decided to roll out Karen's plan. He had brochures made up for the union stewards to distribute at the meetings. Karen's success with the Teamsters encouraged her to approach other unions. The two most notable were the Brotherhood of Electrical Contractors and the Plumbing Union.

ELECTRONIC MARKETING MACHINE

Three years after the establishment of Cornerstone, Becky received a diagnosis of breast cancer. She remained an active participant for an additional four years, but as she was losing her battle to this terrible disease, they decided it was best to sell the company ten years after its inception. Karen treasured Becky's insight and contributions until her passing in 2002.

At the pinnacle of Cornerstone's business, builder clients accounted for a little over 40 percent of their closings, Weiss being the majority contributor from this niche. Another 25–27 percent were generated from corporate accounts, 15–18 percent was the result of apartment complex marketing, and the remaining 15–22 percent came from the closed client customer base.

Right around the time of the sale, Karen's husband took a promotion, which meant the family needed to relocate to Wisconsin. Simultaneously, *Mortgage Originator* magazine (MOM) approached Karen to consider running their Mortgage SuperStars Seminars program. She had been a featured columnist on their site and been on the editorial board for eight years. Karen felt this was right up her alley *and* it allowed her to run her new endeavor—Foundation Marketing—concurrently.

Her firm specialized in consumer-direct pieces that a loan officer could purchase off the shelf. Karen had been refining and updating her materials as needed for the past decade. Originators could literally begin their consumer-direct program immediately upon receiving their shipments.

Soon after starting her new venture, Karen created another business—LoanOfficerTraining.com, one of the first Internet-based companies to provide online training for loan officers (and real estate agents). The company's tagline said it all. "When in-house training is not enough." The product filled a hole for salespeople looking for a unique selling proposition (USP). She created workbooks, audio tapes, and marketing pieces. Initially, purchasers received structured systematic procedures along with the materials provided. Today, LoanOfficerTraining.com also includes webinars, e-zines, and free downloads. Roughly one year after she founded the company, Karen started interviewing top-producing loan officers from around the country. The recordings are available on a subscription basis at a low monthly price. Once again, Karen was a maverick in a virtually non-existent (and now huge) market. If anyone has the ability to know what originators will need to be successful, it's definitely Karen. The next seven years were a busy time for her as she went on to launch five additional companies that fell under Foundation Marketing's umbrella.

- ◆ **ApartmentToolKit.com,** a company Karen recently sold, is a service that provides apartment mailing lists and materials geared towards locating and marketing to first-time homebuyers.

- ◆ **LoanOfficerMagazine.com** is an online e-zine that features sales and marketing articles, tactics, and strategies to help loan originators increase their business. Included in the subscription are downloadable marketing flyers, postcards, charts, and checklists.

- ◆ **MortgageCurrentcy.com** is another venture Karen recently sold. The e-zine interprets how recent mortgage regulations, and the revisions to those rules affect loan officers, processors, underwriters, branch managers, and mortgage company owners.

◆ **MortgageGirlfriends.com** is a website and blogging tool Karen created exclusively for females in the mortgage lending. Women in all facets of the industry including those who represent affiliated businesses benefit from this amazing resource.

◆ **Consumer-Direct-Marketing.com** is a site that's longer active. However, the content has been transferred to the LoanOfficerTraining.com These tools provide originators a way to generate their own leads. It also includes strategic, targeted ads that work, getting the most out of marketing dollars spent.

To understand the level of success Karen has achieved, type her name into the Google search bar. Literally, every single entry on the first two pages is from her or about her. This is remarkable! Similar results happen when you enter products Karen sells, offers, or recommends. In terms of the Internet, she is everywhere. Without a doubt, Karen is an electronic marketing machine.

WOMEN IN THE SPOTLIGHT

For nearly eight years, one of Karen's passion has been to help women in the mortgage industry receive the recognition they deserve for the value they bring to the table. Her book *Stilettos in a Loafer World: Mortgage Women Who Walk Their Talk*, published in late 2008, was the first of several books she's written to spotlight women mortgage professionals. Karen felt that sharing their stories would provide inspiration. This was just the beginning of the next leg of her dynamic career. During an interview for the *National Mortgage News*™ conducted on January 2, 2009, Karen was asked where she got the idea for her book. Karen said it happened when she spoke at an industry conference. "I wanted to know why there were only two women speakers." The response she received was, "We don't know of any other successful women to ask." Karen knew of plenty, and she was sure they did too. It was her belief they chose *not* to have a higher ratio. She continued, "So I decided to start interviewing women, and write a book about how they run their businesses differently and have attained success."

Karen's previous endeavors place her as a pioneer of niche marketing, but none are so near and dear to her heart as supporting female salespeople. She established Mortgage Girlfriends specifically for this reason. Membership includes online resources in the form of articles, educational workshops, networking forums, and chat groups. It also provides a safe environment for members to air challenges while receiving honest feedback and solutions.

Since starting this leg of her professional journey, Karen has held five Mortgage Girlfriends Mastermind conferences, written five books, and been a resource for thousands of subscribers. She took her experience and expertise to create income streams that no longer require her to originate mortgages. That was not her original intention; life just unfolded that way.

Is it possible to need mortgage-related tools that are not from Karen's offerings? While we have a difficult time imagining that, don't worry if she doesn't have what you need. Karen will assist you with a referral. In her own words: "I only recommend seminars, sales tools, and speakers that I believe in, and know to be credible. I do not try to sell you stuff for the sake of making a sale. In fact, I consider myself successful only if my clients are successful."

Over the years, Karen has demonstrated her ability to define a need way ahead of the emerging trends. The result is a composition of tools, trainings, and products that are tested to ensure success for those users who implement them. Now that is impressive. Welcome to Karen Deis's one-stop-shopping in electric stilettos!

NEW TOOLS OF THE TRADE
Social Media Tips

Shared by Kathleen

———————————◄※►—————————————

Once a new technology rolls over you, if you're not part
of the steamroller, you're part of the road.

—STEWART BRAND

THE IMPORTANCE OF database management has been talked about for
years, but rarely has it been implemented at full throttle. Many stop at
contact management, which keeps salespeople in front of the client, but
falls short of tapping into the full value of the customer relationship. The
difference between the two is that database management is the extraction
of data that resides in each record to create more opportunities. A prime
example of tapping into this is when David Jaffe and Julie Miller run a
query to find borrowers whose loan amount has reached conforming
limits. This situation might have occurred because of appreciation or
increased county limits. Another terrific illustration is when Karen Deis
performed a search of all borrowers who worked for particular employers
to obtain their testimonial letters. Tom Ninness dug deeper into his base
when he searched for highly ranked CPAs, Financial Planners, and other
professionals who would add to value to his presentations.

When I worked at American Home, we, too, saw the potential. We hired the illustrious Cindy Douglas in February 2007 for that very reason. We wanted to build the best system we could for our proprietary use to gain market share. The executive team felt the combination of a robust database with the professional pieces developed by AHM's marketing department would get us there.

Some of our more progressive loan officers had started dabbling in Facebook; however, as a company, it wasn't an area we focused on before we closed our doors in 2007. Social media had not taken hold as it has in recent years. I and some of the management team were using LinkedIn, but that was about it. MySpace™ was a hot ticket, but it was definately for personal use, and not professional. For the most part, loan officers and the mortgage companies that employ them still don't have a comprehensive understanding of this medium, and as a result, it remains underutilized.

A frustrating aspect of technology is the speed at which change takes place. The advances that have happened in the ten years since 2008 will be *nothing* compared to where we will be within the next few years. Actually, it's likely that at least one of the social media tools mentioned in this chapter will have changed dramatically by the time I finish typing! Rolling, rolling, rolling . . .

How, then, does a sales professional work magic with this form of connectivity effectively? The short answer is that you use social media to choose social media. But how? That doesn't mean you start and end your search on Google or with consulting the reviews about online tools. That's just the tip of the iceberg. It means setting up accounts on several platforms. Facebook allows you to find out who's doing what, why, and when in the industry. Twitter helps to discern the up and coming trends, see what's attracting traffic, and gain tips that relate to your business. LinkedIn attracts a different type of readership, making it a valuable forum to be active on. All of this is just to perform your *research* and help you generate ideas digitally. After you've formulated a plan, you'll create business pages for all of these platforms to build your presence on the Internet.

WHO'S USING WHAT

When the Pew Research Center started tracking social media adoption in 2005, only 5 percent of American adults used at least one Internet platform. By 2011, that percentile had risen to more than half, and in 2017, usage had reached 69 percent. So how does a loan officer decide which options are the most effective to generate business? By studying the demographics. For example, take a look at these statistics from Pew Research's November 2016 Social Media Update:[1]

- 79 percent of adults online, or 68 percent of the entire adult population, use Facebook.

- 31 percent of adults online, or 26 percent of the entire adult population, use Pinterest.

- 32 percent of adults online, or 28 percent of the entire adult population, use Instagram.

- 29 percent of adults online, or 25 percent of the entire adult population, use LinkedIn.

- 24 percent of adults online, or 21 percent of the entire adult population, use Twitter.

Facebook far surpasses the other social media platforms at 79 percent. The data further shows that the younger the generation, the more likely they are to use Facebook; just look at the statistics:

- 88 percent of those from ages eighteen to twenty-nine.

- 84 percent of those from ages thirty to forty-nine.

- 72 percent of those from ages fifty to sixty-four.

- 62 percent of those sixty-five and older.

How does this information help? Suppose an originator decides to concentrate on first-time homebuyers. They have chosen down payment assistance as their core niche product to tap into this market. If the research indicates that a large majority of people in their early thirties are first-time buyers, then Facebook is a good place to start a targeted campaign. Why? Because 84 percent of people aged thirty to forty-nine are actively engaged on this platform. But wait, not so fast. There's more information to consider. According to the same update:

- Multi-platform use is on the rise: More than 56 percent of online adults now use two or more social media sites, compared to 42 percent of Internet users in 2013.

- Young adults ages eighteen to twenty-nine are the most active users on Instagram at 59 percent. As in previous PEW Research Center surveys, 38 percent of women are more likely to use Instagram versus percent of men.

- LinkedIn is primarily used by college graduates. The other group that taps into this aspect of social media is wage earners with annual incomes of $75,000 or more. 50 percent of online adults access this medium.

- Women dominate Pinterest at 45 percent versus 17 percent of men. Pinterest has captured 32 percent of the online market share.

Another point worth considering is the popularity of Snapchat", more popular than Twitter among millennials with a 32.9 percent penetration on the demographics' mobile phones.[2] So if this is your target market you'd want to take into account how they use their phones. This will help you to figure out the best way to message your communications to them; should it be text, e-mail, or voicemail.

The *Social Media Examiner* found similar results with their 2016 survey.[3] Rather than the public, they queried marketers. Their findings indicated that the amount of time spent online directly influences the percentage of focus time that should be spent in a particular social media platform. Due to the amount and the complexity of data regarding social media, many salespeople today are hiring consultants who specialize in this area to work with them. Some are taking classes to learn how to best use this form, while others are employed by a company that does this step for them.

If you're an Internet master (such as Karen Deis and others featured in this book), it might make sense to just skim the rest of this chapter. Otherwise, for those seeking initial social media guidance or looking for a new idea or want to dust an old one off, here are some tips that may be of assistance.

◆ Your company may have a policy regarding what you can post to LinkedIn, Facebook, or Twitter. Make sure you follow protocol before launching and posting in these arenas. To make the most out of your business contacts, write articles that are of interest to them. Add short, clean jokes or inspirational quotes. Include mortgage news that may affect your clients and/or service providers. Always remember that people, including clients, prospects, and sources of business *will* run a search to find you. They will often see everything you post. So take care with the social content you choose to write about, the pictures you upload, and the extracurricular activities that you associate yourself with on your personal account. It's fine to post family updates and photos of you, your spouse, kids, and pets on this page, just be prudent.

◆ Join groups. There are literally thousands of them on LinkedIn alone. Set up e-mail notifications to alert you about new posts from members after you join. Whether you use Microsoft® Outlook, Gmail, or one of the other e-mail systems, you can easily establish a rule to send these posts to a "read later" folder (and then remember to read these). Another option is to forward these posts to a different e-mail address that you can only access at home, reviewing them during your down time. Another alternative is to have your assistant perform a once-over, providing you with the Cliffs Notes, or whatever works best for you. I recommend contributing to these groups as applicable to add to your credibility while complying within your company regulations.

◆ If your company has pages on any social media platform, be sure to add these to your personal sites, your business cards, your e-mail address signatures, and so on. Most people *will* search you on the Internet after they have met you or received your name as a referral. Be sure what they see is professional, positive, informative, relevant, entertaining, and helpful.

◆ On that note, remember to Google yourself a few times a year. This may yield very good results, or even distressing information. While you may not have heard back from that disgruntled client, he or she may create a review. It's very common for them to have gone directly to Yelp™ or the Better Business Bureau. A tarnished web presence can cause irreparable damage. Your company may already have someone who is designated to perform this search for all employees, but even if they do it's still a good idea to check yourself or delegate this process effectively. Staying informed about what others are saying about you is important. It provides insight about how you are perceived.

◆ Be the geographical social media market expert. Post items of interest about your city, county, or state.

◆ Based on the statistics in the beginning of this chapter, use Snapchat to source millennials. Users can take pictures, record videos, add words and drawings, and send them to a specified list of recipients.

◆ If your target clientele is in the older age bracket and they are looking to move-up or downsize, focus on Facebook; they seem to favor that platform more than the other social media options.

◆ Create "wow" charts, presentations, and numerical examples, using a tool like The Mortgage Coach®. It's a great way to create a professional looking presentation, and demonstrate your level of expertise. (http://mortgagecoach.com/)

◆ Go low-tech too. Consider using a tool such as SlyDial™ when you want to leave a voicemail message on a client's cell phone without having their phone ring. David Jaffe has had great results using this product. (https://www.slydial.com/)

- There are literally hundreds of other tools depending on what you want to do, for whom, when, and how often. For example:

  - Hootsuite™ lets you schedule postings to any of your social media sites at a pre-determined time and does tons of other things for you. (https://hootsuite.com/)
  - MailChimp is an online e-mail marketing solution to manage contacts, send e-mails, and track results. It also creates slick newsletters. (http://mailchimp.com/)
  - Constant Contact™ is another system that sends e-mail blasts to your customer base. You'll be able to analyze which topics create interest and which ones don't. This will help you to write content that generates a higher response rate. (https://www.constantcontact.com)

Those are just three I've personally used and have some working knowledge of. Each offers a free version, but the feature sets are limited until the user elects to pay the subscription fee. While there are an abundance of tools and services out there to help promote your business, these three recommendations came from co-workers, friends in the industry, and technically savvy acquaintances of mine. I have a simple process before implementing a new technology. When I am given a recommendation, I investigate the suggestion. If I think it makes sense, I move forward. I have found this is the best route to follow because it saves time and money. Instead of hoping your investment pays off you'll already know of at least one person if not more who have already had success.

MORE TECH OPTIONS

Here are some other activities, tools, and strategies you may want or need to consider:

- **Blogging.** At the time of this writing, there are literally several hundred million blogs in the world. So why become a small fish in a very, very large ocean? Because there are some positive things to consider.

- Having a blog associated with your name, team, or company increases visibility in search results, as long as you word your blog content carefully and appropriately.
- Blogs can convert readers into clients. If your post contains the popular hooking type of content, it will direct readers from other social media sites like Facebook and Twitter to where your blog resides, increasing your potential lead base significantly.
- In most cases, blogs are interactive, which means you're able to get instant feedback, opinions, and engagement from existing and potential clients. This is very powerful for establishing and maintaining your personal brand. This is exactly what Michael Deery and Larry Bettag have done.

  A word of advice: use the Four Eyes review process before posting. Poorly written blogs in terms of spelling, grammar, clarity, and/or that has content that could be construed as offensive can have major negative effects on you and your organization. This is why it's a good idea to have a minimum of two people review for you.
- You could also contribute to a blog other than your own. For example, I currently contribute an article to ratezip.com's blog. It is a great way for me to become associated with their clients with minimal effort on my part.

♦ **Webinars.** Conducting or participating in video conferences on a computer or mobile device is an excellent way to stay in front of your customer base. The content can be delivered live, on-demand, or an off-the-rack version that you purchase. Webinar providers such as GoToMeeting™, WebEx™, and Zoom are just a few of the numerous choices out there.

♦ **ActiveRain.** This forum is made up of a community of real estate professionals and other related fields. The platform provides bloggers with an avenue to market themselves, gain referrals, and expand their business. Its a terrific way to connect, share, and learn from each other, while also educating the consumer.

◆ **Google Drive and Dropbox.** The beauty of these cloud-based systems is you and someone else can be on different computers and working on the same file, whether you are in the same location or not. With Google Drive and Dropbox (if you're using Microsoft® Office 365), you can even collaborate in real time, at the same time. Apple iCloud and Microsoft® OneDrive™ are two other similar online storage tools, with many more out there.

◆ **Databases.** Has your company contracted with Salesforce™ or a product with similar attributes? If not have you implemented your own program such as Vantage or the Media Center? If not, be certain you do. It's imperative to keep track electronically of *every single one* of your clients, leads, and sources of business. Keeping the database up to date is important, but it's not enough; it must trigger notifications to alert you when the customer's existing interest rate is anywhere from .5 to 1 percent or higher than the current market, depending on the loan size. Knowing their birthdays, when children are most likely ready to leave the nest, and the other important milestones we've discussed is critical for client retention.

A former employer of mine surveyed the top 5 percent of mortgage loan originators and learned that more than 80 percent of their business came to them from their closed clients. It's possible they got lucky and these borrowers remembered their contact information, but it's not probable. More likely, the loan officer did a really good job of staying in touch, yielding hundreds of new loans for themselves and the organization. One last note about the database: be certain you know for sure, who owns it, you or your company.

◆ **Proprietary tools.** Be sure to ask your employer if they offer streamlined digital platforms that provide a collaborative portal for borrowers and real estate professionals, such as Floify.™ This product along with numerous others keep customers and partners in-the-loop with milestone updates. It's worth investigating to see how you and your clientele can benefit most from these types of mortgage products.

- **Smartphones.** Take everything I've covered in this chapter and the eight zillion other tools not mentioned and make sure they're all compatible with your current smartphone or the model you are considering before you purchase the device. That's right, another search: "Where are those apps I want to use and do they work on my phone?" If a tool only works on your laptop or desktop, unfortunately, it's already *way* out of date.

Let's wrap up by discussing some things that you should *not* do when using social networking. To emphasize some points discussed in this chapter, I'm summarizing an article I found through a LinkedIn update: "4 Ways Salespeople Get Social Networking Wrong" by Joanne Black.[4]

1. **Cold calling.** Don't ask people to connect with you for the sole purpose of sending sales offers.

2. **Asking for referrals.** Don't ask a person for a referral on social media if that platform is the entire basis of your relationship. People refer only those they like and trust. If you don't know the individual well enough to pick up the phone, the status of your relationship doesn't merit the request.

3. **Forgetting to nurture your network.** Once you earn trust and friendship on the Internet, it's imperative to continue to engage. Remember to stay in touch, interact, offer assistance, and extend invitations to groups.

4. **Being too social to socialize.** In other words, sales isn't a party. Don't just grow your network; make sure to nurture it. Put in the time and effort online. The goal is to create offline conversations, in order to build connections that count.

Now, go make some magic!

ACKNOWLEDGMENTS

———————— ❧ ————————

WE WOULD LIKE TO THANK all the people who allowed their names to be included in our book. Without them, the content would not have been nearly as valuable and rich.

Our interviewees, in sequential order: Greg Frost, Drew McKenzie, David Jaffe, Jeff Lake, Julie Miller, Larry Bettag, Michael Deery, Mike Smalley, Ralph Massella, Tom Ninness, Mark Raskin, and Karen Deis. You've been beyond generous.

Those who allowed their names to enhance the message, in sequential order: Todd Duncan, Tom Le Master, Irma McChristy, Linda Farris, Kate Wilson, Jed Herman, Cindy Herman, Holly St. Germain, Linda Goland, John Manglardi, Jo Ann Theriault-Fazio, Deanna Valeo, Alison Bond, Ivette Reynoso, Melissa Johnston, Mike Gulitz, Stacey Harding, Hallie Palacios, Nancy Smith, Tim Braheem, Aaron Ninness, Cathy Stroud, Seychelle Van Poole Engelhard, Chris Nooney, Bill Hart, and Jenna Lindseth.

Thank you to Susan Hartsock for her feedback before the book came to life, Rob Chrisman and Duane Gomer for their counsel as the work got closer to completion. Chloe Hecht, Senior Counsel, and Mary Newill, Administrative Assistant for the National Association of REALTORS®, for their assistance the usage of the the REALTOR® trademark; and our families for tolerating the hours spent.

Cindy and Kathleen

REFERENCES

---◆※◆---

TEACH, ADAPT, LEARN: BE TAL!

[1] U.S. Office of Housing and Urban Development, "Analysis of the Florida Housing Market," (as of April, 2003). https://www.huduser.gov/publications/pdf/CMAR_Orlando.pdf

[2] The Senate Committee on Appropriations, The House Appropriations Committee, and The Legislative Office of Economic and Demographic Research, "State of Florida Long Range Financial Outlook, Fiscal Years 2017–18 and 2019–20." www.leg.state.fl.us/data/committees/joint/jlbc/Long%20RangeFinancialOutlook2017-18_1920.pdf.

KNOW THE CLEANING LADY: BUILD A STRONG FAMILY CULTURE

[1] "Prime Lending Sales Rally 2012," https://www.youtube.com/watch?v=cJRowH7dGSs.

NEW TOOLS OF THE TRADE

[1] Shannon Greenwood, Andrew Perrin, and Mave Duggan, "Social Media Update 2016," Pew Research Center, November 11, 2016. http://www.pewinternet.org/2016/11/11/social-media-update-2016.

[2] Martin-Wilbourn Partners. "Snapchat Is Now the Third Most Popular Social Network among Millennials." http://mwpartners.com/snapchat-is-now-the-third-most-popular-social-network-among-millennials.

[3] *Social Media Examiner.* "2016 Social Media Marketing Report." https://www.socialmediaexaminer.com/social-media-marketing-industry-report-2016.

[4] Joanne Black. "4 Ways Salespeople Get Social Networking Wrong," No More Cold Calling, www.nomorecoldcalling.com/4-ways-salespeople-get-social-networking-wrong.

INTERVIEW QUESTIONS FOR MORTGAGE RETAIL SALES

With Some Analysis

—◆※◆—

I was in a job interview today when the manager handed me his
laptop and said, "I want you to try and sell this to me."
So I put it under my arm, walked out of the building, and went home.
Eventually he called my mobile and said,
"Bring it back here right now!" I said, "$1000 and it's yours."

RECRUIT'S NAME: _____

CURRENT EMPLOYER: _____

CURRENT MANAGER: _____

NOTES ON INTERNET CHECK OF RECRUIT: *(Google, Facebook, LinkedIn, etc.)*

_____

_____

_____

_____

Clear these questions with your Human Resource Director before using them as state laws vary.

SPECIFIC BUSINESS QUESTIONS		
QUESTION:	GOOD FIT RESPONSES:	RED FLAG RESPONSES:
Tell me the percentage breakdown of your business by loan type.	If this matches the products your company has or wants, continue.	▪ High jumbo percentage when your organization doesn't offer the product or have a conduit to be competitive. ▪ High government production when you don't have the underwriting expertise to close that business.
How many leads do you have right now? How many of them are pre-approvals or pre-qualifications? Where did you source these leads?	▪ Anyone can state a high number of leads. Pre-qualifications/Pre-approvals can be documented (ask for that). ▪ Pay particular attention to how they generate leads to ensure it matches your corporate business model.	If all their leads are purchased from a list or from an Internet lead generation company and you want self-sourced external books of business, this may not be a fit.
What was your [last calendar year] closed loan volume—in units and dollars?	The individual is able to document their numbers and they meet or exceed your company standard for closed loan volume, then good!	If the person is below standards, probe to find out why. If nothing compelling stands out, this hire is most likely a bad risk.
What geography do you cover?	Look for a match of where you need coverage; check for overlap with existing, performing staff.	"The entire U.S."—if you seek an external salesperson for a specific geography, or if you are not licensed nationally, this may not be a fit for either party.
How are you currently paid?	The best candidate is one who is currently paid similarly to how you pay.	Listen for non-compliant or extraordinary commissions, bonuses, etc. If they are paid way above the industry average, find out why they are leaving.
Tell me about your mortgage experience.	Looking for positive movement and success with reputable lenders.	Job hopping, association with companies that have questionable reputations, gaps of employment, etc.
What is your current pipeline and what will happen to it if you leave?	▪ You want to hear about a healthy pipeline, and you want a person who knows his/her numbers. ▪ They have an ethical exit plan to have files close without him/her there.	▪ The candidate indicates a low pipeline, and doesn't know or is evasive about his/her numbers. ▪ The candidate who says he/she will "bring it all with him/her" (illegal—unless the customer chooses that option, in writing).

Clear these questions with your Human Resource Director before using them as state laws vary.

SPECIFIC BUSINESS QUESTIONS		
QUESTION:	GOOD FIT RESPONSES:	RED FLAG RESPONSES:
Is there anyone at your existing company you would like to bring with you?	Good answers include other salespeople, operations staff, and some management.	Less positive replies include: "no one," "no," etc. Probe the "why?"
Who are your top real estate agents, builders, financial planners?	The best responses include recognizable names, and sources that match the company's model.	Unfavorable responses include a lack of or unknown names, much hesitation, responding "no" without an acceptable explanation, etc.
How much did you make last year and how much do you want to make this year?	■ Best: Stated without hesitation with projections for increased income. ■ Okay: Decreased slightly/stable income with a logical and acceptable explanation, with steps in place to increase earnings.	■ Declining income without a reasonable explanation. ■ Explanations based on being a victim or blaming others.
How many names do you have in your database and how do you use it?	High numbers and an effective contact management plan.	None or wouldn't see the value of having a database if the company didn't supply.
What is your application to closing ratio?	The higher the number, the better.	Low percentages or doesn't know.
How do you quote rates?	■ Asks several relevant questions first before quoting rates. ■ Has an effective and well thought out process to lock "floating rate" clients. ■ Demonstrates a clear understanding of the customer's appetite for risk before going through the pros/cons of floating versus locking the rate.	■ Quotes directly from the rate sheet without going over different options. ■ Quotes rates lower than they really are to get the deal in the door. ■ Locks everyone at application without going over the options because it is easier.
Tell me the income you earned in your best year ever and what year was that?	High and recent are best.	Low or declining income.

Clear these questions with your Human Resource Director before using them as state laws vary.

SPECIFIC BUSINESS QUESTIONS		
QUESTION:	GOOD FIT RESPONSES:	RED FLAG RESPONSES:
How were you trained to be a mortgage professional? What do you do to stay abreast of current issues, opportunities, etc. in the industry?	Question #1: The individual has been through a training program, mentorship or are at least self-taught with a plan and process. Question #2: The recruit attends industry conferences, sales seminars, etc.	Question #1: The individual has no training, has not gone through a mentorship program, and has not taken the initiative to be self-taught. Question #2: The individual doesn't see the value.
How do you use social media? What works most effectively for you?	Listen for a well thought out strategy and the implementation of an effective plan that is driven by results.	No use of social media.
What kind of goals motivate you the best?	Listen for what you personally seek—volume goals, income goals, etc.	None or a negative response.
Tell me about your current team.	Listen for pride in team members such as assistants, operations staff, partners, etc.	They consider themselves a lone wolf.
Exactly how do you generate leads?	The individual has an effective process matching what you seek—leads from real estate agents and builders, for example.	There is no process in place or waits for the phone to ring.
We perform a full background check and credit check. Do you anticipate any problem with that?	Candidate has no concerns	There are issues without mitigating circumstances that are acceptable to the company.

Interview Questions for Mortgage Retail Sales

Clear these questions with your Human Resource Director before using them as state laws vary.

OPEN PROBE SUBJECTIVE INTERVIEW QUESTIONS

QUESTION:	GOOD FIT RESPONSES:	RED FLAG RESPONSES:
What kind of opportunity would compel you to work here?	Listen for what the candidate wants or needs. Ask yourself if you're able to provide the tools/climate that creates the opportunity for this person.	An obvious red flag—needing/wanting more base compensation than you offer or anything else that you will not or cannot provide.
What has to happen in one year for you to feel excited about your success?	Listen for comments about their volume and personal growth with an emphasis on what is realistically attainable here. Is their definition of success aligned with what benefits you, the team, and the company?	If there is little chance that what the person describes can/will happen here, proceed very cautiously. Also listen for things that describe traits you do NOT want to hire— dishonesty, inflexibility, no commitment to excellence, etc.
Tell me the pros and cons of working completely on your own.	Listen for statements that demonstrate initiative. For example, "I like establishing my own weekly schedule and accomplishing all the goals I have listed on it."	Candidates that aren't self-motivated, or rely on someone else to do most of the work. For example, their assistant handles the majority of the customer interface or they expect their management to handle all operational issues.
Have you ever or do you now participate in sports? Tell me about that.	Best: Yes and comments about activities that require discipline, planning, a good work ethic, a focus on team efforts, etc.	No and never: Find out if this is from a lack of interest on their part and why. Not all who are disinterested in sports are bad hires. However, it could be an indication of qualities that are not a fit.
What do you do for fun?	Activities that demonstrate balance, family values, health, etc.	Activities that may be counterproductive to success—gambling, partying, etc.
What was your first job?	▪ Is it entrepreneurial in nature. For example a paper route, lemonade stand etc. ▪ See if the experience has translated into subsequent success. ▪ Find out what prompted them to apply for this job.	▪ If this is their first job, and you don't have a successful rookie program, this may not be a win-win for either party. ▪ If the job started later in life than is considered typical, probe deeper. ▪ If the job was not long ago and radically different, probe extensively.
Tell me how you handle the three most common objections you get.	The individual asks open-ended questions, identifies the customer's pain points, and then offers solutions. They subscribe to the 80/20 principle. 80 percent listening and 20 percent of the time speaking.	The person shows signs of call reluctance, has low conversion rates or relies on someone else to close the deal for them.

Clear these questions with your Human Resource Director before using them as state laws vary.

OPEN PROBE SUBJECTIVE INTERVIEW QUESTIONS

QUESTION:	GOOD FIT RESPONSES:	RED FLAG RESPONSES:
What do you like about the mortgage industry? What would you change?	▪ Focuses on the positive. ▪ Has well thought out solutions for change.	▪ Doesn't like the job; indicates it's a way to make a living. ▪ Hasn't thought about, or only complains.
What book are you reading and why?	Listen for books that somehow assist with self-improvement.	Prioritizes activities in their spare time that prevents them from reading and doesn't promote growth.
Tell me about a time you feel like you failed. What do you do when you lose?	▪ Listen for the "picked myself up afterwards" aspect of this response. ▪ Demonstrates the ability to learn and implement.	▪ Blames everyone else for their failings. ▪ Demonstrates a defeatist or victim mentality.
Tell me about a time you WON.	This question is trying to discern competitiveness. Big wins are better—for example, winning the national baseball championship in college versus a spelling bee in fifth grade.	Small wins may indicate low levels of competitiveness. Pay attention to wins that do not fit your culture—for instance, winning a fight for a huge loan but having omitted or disregarded certain facts to make it happen.
Suppose things worked out well between us and you joined us. Tell me about your first week —what do you expect you will be doing each day?	A good response would be, "What requirements would you have of me?" Also good is if they have the desire to hit the ground running—to tell everyone about his/her new company.	If the person seeks structured, in-class training in an offsite location— and that is not the case here. If the person says he/she will not be doing much for a few months while learning takes place, proceed with caution.
Of all your accomplishments, tell me about the one that makes you the most proud.	Listen for accomplishments that meet your needs and indicate that the candidate has several of the desired traits you seek.	If the accomplishments stated would not have made you, anyone on your team, or most people at the company proud, proceed with caution.
Jump ahead three years. Tell me all about your professional life then.	A good answer is one that includes how they will grow professionally and how that equates to the income they plan to earn. It is ideal if the recruit visualizes that happening as an employee at your company.	Do their future objectives align with the company's direction? If the person is looking to move-on from the role you are hiring them for and it's not a fit reconsider moving forward.

Clear these questions with your Human Resource Director before using them as state laws vary.

OPEN PROBE SUBJECTIVE INTERVIEW QUESTIONS		
QUESTION:	**GOOD FIT RESPONSES:**	**RED FLAG RESPONSES:**
How does your greatest strength help you succeed?	The key here is learning the recruit's perception of his/her greatest strength. Seek those that mirror traits you know are correlated to success.	Listen for qualities that fall into the liability column for the job you're hiring for. Examples in the sales role are: shyness, the desire to work alone, ruthlessness, lack of persistence, etc.
What do you do to ensure excellent customer service?	Listen for quick and consistent responsiveness, upfront preparation and communication, performing client needs analysis, setting realistic expectations, etc.	Responses that imply good customer service is someone else's responsibility or the applicant doesn't rank as a high priority, has a tendency to wing-it, over promise, etc.
Who inspires you and why?	Pay attention to the traits of the individual they admire and see if they echo those you desire.	If the qualities mentioned in the "why" conflict with what you're looking for, the individual may not be a good fit.
What are your top three skills? What three do you need assistance, delegation or training on?	Goes to self-awareness. Is the person able to clearly articulate their strengths and weaknesses? Is the individual able to identify which skills sets they should have more training in, and which ones are better off being delegated and why?	Responses shouldn't be general or vague. For example, "I am a people person" doesn't provide substance. Are the areas the individual is lacking talent required for the position? Do they have a tough time delegating, which in turn impacts their ability to spend time on the core responsibilities of the position you're hiring for.
What can you tell or teach me that you're sure I don't know?	• Does the person ask you probing questions? • Do they think before responding?	• The individual doesn't ask open-ended questions. • They're answers lack relevancy.
Why do you succeed?	Answer includes traits and activities over which the recruit has control—responsiveness, honesty, knowledge, hard work, confidence, diligence, etc.	Response does not indicate self-motivation/initiative. The person is reliant on outside factors to propel them forward.

Clear these questions with your Human Resource Director before using them as state laws vary.

OPEN PROBE SUBJECTIVE INTERVIEW QUESTIONS

QUESTION:	GOOD FIT RESPONSES:	RED FLAG RESPONSES:
Tell me about the best and worst team you have ever worked with.	If the best description epitomizes your team—excellent. If they define the worst as being opposite of yours—also excellent.	If the best describes a team that doesn't fit your culture, one you don't have, nor would ever want to have— red flag. If the worst describes your team—also a red flag.
Describe the best manager, teacher, or coach you ever had and why he/she ranks as best.	Responses that describe the managerial style of the person they will report to—particularly if the rationale behind the high ranking has been a successful recipe for personal growth.	If their best describes a managerial style you don't have or don't subscribe to—red flag. If the worst describes you or the person they will report to, most likely this will not be a good fit.
Tell me about the best job or class you ever had and why it was best.	If they are animated in their replies and the attributes embody what will be expected of them—outstanding.	If it appears they are rattling off what you want to hear or they lack enthusiasm it could be an indication that the position isn't right for the individual.
What motivates you?	Answers that include happy clients, earning a high income, reward for hard work, appreciation, and/or things you will be able to provide.	Responses that are counter-productive or the motivation is questionable—such as always being right, setting their own hours so they can leave early etc.
Tell me about the last time you were angry and what happened because of that?	What caused the anger is less important than how it was handled. Listen for solutions that led to the greater good—such as satisfied customers, great team work, improved relationships with co-workers, etc.	Pay attention to the end result. Did it cause them to resign, a deterioration in communication, poor customer service, etc. Be sure to ask many more questions.
What kind of work environment is best for you?	If the recruit describes your work environment, excellent!	If the recruit describes the opposite culture of your work environment, proceed with caution and get more details.
What five positive adjectives do people use to describe you? Negative?	Listen for traits you seek. Determine if the negative qualities are positive characteristics for the job.	If these aren't the attributes you are seeking delve deeper to determine if there's a fit.

Clear these questions with your Human Resource Director before using them as state laws vary.

OPEN PROBE SUBJECTIVE INTERVIEW QUESTIONS		
QUESTION:	GOOD FIT RESPONSES:	RED FLAG RESPONSES:
Tell me about a time you definitely provided service beyond expectations.	If you like how the recruit did this, great.	Listen for a recruit who comes across as always being the hero. Dig deeper to ascertain if that person creates and/or magnifies the problem and then solves it. This could be a red flag.
Describe the most innovative approach you have ever used to solve a problem.	Listen carefully and see how this solution would fit into your work environment.	Plenty of opportunity for red flags here. Does their innovative approach border on crossing the line? Does it appear their motivation is strictly for personal financial gain?
What do you fear the most, professionally?	Good answers may include not being able to meet the clients' needs, not having an open relationship with management, or a company that lacks a positive culture, etc.	Listen for fears that may manifest themselves at your company because of similar environments or management styles.

Check with your Human Resources department for other questions that are prohibited by state law.

INTERVIEW QUESTIONS YOU *CANNOT* ASK

BACKGROUND:	TOPICS TO AVOID	ASK INSTEAD:
Employers are prohibited from using the answers from some of the following criteria to determine employment:	• Race	• Are you authorized to work in the US?
	• Native language	• What languages do you read or speak fluently?
	• Birth place	
• Age	• Marital status	• Have you worked or earned a degree under another name?
• Race	• Desire to have children	• Are you able to start work at 8 a.m.?
• Color	• Parental status	• What days are you available to work?
• Sex	• Commuting distance	• Are you willing to relocate?
• National origin	• Age	• Are you able to perform the specific duties of this position?
• Birthplace	• Height and weight	
• Marital status	• Chronic illness	• How many days of work did you miss last year?
• Religion	• Disabilities	• Are you able to perform the essential functions of this job with or without reasonable accommodations?
• Disability	• Religious beliefs	
It is important to understand what constitutes an illegal question versus a legal question. For example, the interviewer is not permitted to ask when a recruit was born, however they are permitted to ask if the person is over age eighteen or other minimum age requirements. Similarly, employers cannot discriminate against disabled persons; however, they can ask whether an applicant can physically perform essential job tasks.	• Parents' background	• Have you ever been convicted of a felony?
	• Arrest record (in general—see right)	• Have you ever been disciplined for your behavior at work?
	• Willingness to manage or work with teams of men, women, or both	• In the past, have you been disciplined for violating company policies forbidding the use of alcohol or tobacco products?
	• Use of alcohol or tobacco	• Are you a member of a professional or trade group that is relevant to our industry?
	• Club or social organization membership	• Do you have any upcoming events that would require extensive time away from work?
	• National Guard status	• What are your long-term career goals?
The laws in place were designed to reduce or eliminate discrimination and protect the rights of individuals seeking employment. The person conducting the interview should be aware of what questions are permitted and those that are not allowed.		• Are you available to work overtime on occasion?
		• Are you able to travel?

BOOKS AND ARTICLES
ABOUT THE MORTGAGE CRISIS

———————————————◆◈◆———————————————

THERE ARE LITERALLY hundreds of books and thousands more scholarly papers or articles written about the mortgage crisis. Here is a brief list of just a few of them.

BOOKS ABOUT THE MORTGAGE CRISIS

◆ *The Financial Crisis Inquiry Report, Authorized Edition: Final Report of the National Commission on the Causes of the Financial and Economic Crisis in the United States* (New York: PublicAffairs, 2010).

◆ Eduardo Baez and Katrina Kuntz, *Meltdown: I Need a Plan* (Denver: 2009 by Outskirts Press, 2009).

◆ Jack Guttentag, *The Mortgage Encyclopedia: The Authoritative Guide to Mortgage Programs, Practices, Prices and Pitfalls, Second Edition* (New York: McGraw-Hill Education, 2010).

◆ James R. Hagerty, *The Fateful History of Fannie Mae: New Deal Birth to Mortgage Crisis Fall* (Amazon Digital Services, 2012).

◆ Timothy Howard, *The Mortgage Wars: Inside Fannie Mae, Big-Money Politics, and the Collapse of the American Dream (New York:* McGraw-Hill, 2013).

- Dan Immergluck, *Preventing the Next Mortgage Crisis: The Meltdown, the Federal Response, and the Future of Housing in America* (Lanham: Rowman & Littlefield Publishers, 2015).

- Michael Lewis, *The Big Short: Inside the Doomsday Machine,* (New York: W. W. Norton & Company, 2010).

- Bethany McLean and Joe Nocera, *All the Devils Are Here: The Hidden History of the Financial Crisis* (New York: Portfolio, 2011).

- Gretchen Morgenson and Joshua Rosner, *Reckless Endangerment: How Outsized Ambition, Greed, and Corruption Led to Economic Armageddon* (New York: Times Books, 2011).

- Marvin M. Smith and Susan M. Wachter, *The American Mortgage System: Crisis and Reform (The City in the Twenty-First Century)* (Philadelphia: University of Pennsylvania Press, 2014).

- Andrew Ross Sorkin, *Too Big to Fail: The Inside Story of How Wall Street and Washington Fought to Save the Financial System from Crisis—and Themselves* (New York: Viking, 2009).

- Peter Wallison, *Hidden in Plain Sight: What Really Caused the World's Worst Financial Crisis and Why It Could Happen Again* (New York: Encounter Books, 2015).

ARTICLES ABOUT THE MORTGAGE CRISIS

- John Carney, "How the Government Caused the Mortgage Crisis," *Business Insider*, October 16, 2009, http://www.businessinsider.com/how-the-government-caused-the-mortgage-crisis-2009-10.

- Steve Demming, "Lest We Forget: Why We Had a Financial Crisis," *Forbes*, November 22, 2011, https://www.forbes.com/sites/stevedenning/2011/11/22/5086/#5142215af92f.

- Phil Gramm and Mike Solon, "The Clinton-Era Roots of the Financial Crisis," *The Wall Street Journal*, August 12, 2013, https://www.wsj.com/articles/the-clintonera-roots-of-the-financial-crisis-1376348141.

- Leslie Marshall, "Greed Caused the Subprime Mortgage Crisis, not ACORN," *U.S. News*, October 16, 2009, https://www.usnews.com/opinion/articles/2009/10/16/greed-caused-the-subprime-mortgage-crisis-not-acorn.

- Schools Brief, "The Origins of the Financial Crisis," *The Economist*, September 7, 2013, https://www.economist.com/news/schoolsbrief/21584534-effects-financial-crisis-are-still-being-felt-five-years-article.

- Jerome A. Paris, "When did the financial crisis really start?," *Daily Kos*, February 12, 2009, https://www.dailykos.com/stories/2009/2/12/696617/-.

- Azi Paybarah, "Bloomberg: 'Plain and simple,' Congress Caused the Mortgage Crisis, Not the Banks," *Politico*, November, 1, 2011, https://www.politico.com/states/new-york/albany/story/2011/11/bloomberg-plain-and-simple-congress-caused-the-mortgage-crisis-not-the-banks-000000.

- Peter J. Wallison, "The True Origins of This Financial Crisis," *American Spectator*, February 6, 2009, https://spectator.org/42211_true-origins-financial-crisis.

ABOUT THE AUTHORS

CINDY DOUGLAS has been in the mortgage industry for more than thirty years. She founded three companies, most recently Cindy Douglas & Associates. She consults for mortgage companies and originators featured in the nations Top 200, and has assisted a credit union with 100,000+ members with building their real estate lending department from the ground up. Cindy is a recognized national speaker and author.

KATHLEEN HECK is President of the Croyance Group, where she coaches executives, consults with financial companies, and recruits top talent. A former executive vice president of a top ten lender and an executive at several other highly ranked mortgage companies, Kathleen is also the author of two well-received novels, a monthly blog, and motivational posts galore.